GARDENING
FOR THE
ZOMBIE
APOCALYPSE

HOW TO GROW YOUR OWN FOOD
WHEN CIVILIZATION COLLAPSES –
OR EVEN IF IT DOESN'T

ISABEL LLOYD & PHIL CLARKE

HEAD
ZEUS

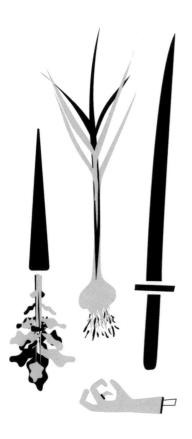

HOW TO USE THIS BOOK

We have a confession to make. A decade ago, when we began growing our own food, we were useless at it. If the apocalypse had started, we'd have been dead within two years.

While we're much better at growing veg now, we're still not experts. So we've tried to make sure that the facts we share with you in this book are backed up by reliable, verifiable sources: peer-reviewed academic papers, university extension programs and government statistics. For example:

- We've based nutritional information on the United States' Department of Agriculture (USDA) Food Composition Databases and the UK government's Guideline Daily Recommendations (GDR).[1]
- Our advice about how many plants to grow per square metre and what amount of crops to expect are based on figures published by the Royal Horticultural Society (RHS) and the Department for Environment, Food and Rural Affairs (DEFRA).[2]
- Information about how to sow, grow and feed plants is based on guidance published by the RHS, the Irish and UK governments and various academic institutions and research groups around the world – with the occasional dash of our own hard-won experience.

You can find a full, numbered breakdown of all our sources, and how we've used them, in the References section.

As for the rest of the book, we know many of you won't have gardened before. So we've tried to be really specific with all the sowing and growing advice we give, which we hope will help you avoid making many of our early mistakes. We also debunk some of the most common and unhelpful gardening myths (look for 'Zombies Are True, This Isn't' boxes) and – if we have to use it – explain any garden jargon and techspeak as clearly as possible (look for words and phrases in green). We've created handy tables to help you get a handle on more complicated information, like how rotation works or what different kinds of fertilizers to use and when. And all the way through you'll find 'Preps for the Pre-Apocalypse', which will give even those of you without a garden advice on how to practise your food-growing skills while civilization still stands.

One last thing before we get started. Gardening is subject to so many variables – soil, weather, the person doing the gardening – that there are never any guarantees. Following the advice here will help you survive the apocalypse. But you should still be ready to develop your own ways of doing things to suit you and your site. And if that doesn't work: don't blame us, blame the zombies.

— Isabel Lloyd & Phil Clarke

INTRODUCTION

When the zombies start stumbling over the hill – and we all know they're on their way – what's the first weapon you should grab? A garden fork. Preferably forged from a single piece of steel. Not because, given a good enough shove, its prongs would pierce a zombie's skull as easily as an overripe melon, but because come the end of the world, gardening will be what saves us.

Why would we say that? Well, firstly because we're a pair of baby boomers who know we've ruined everything for millennials. We're aware that the end may be, if not nigh, then quite a bit nigher than it was. Climate change, Brexit, zombies – something's going to get us. So after ten years teaching ourselves how to grow our own food, we thought it was time we gave a little back and showed you guys how to do it too. Unlike us, you might not have experienced state-funded tertiary education, a viable health service or a functioning housing market, but you can at least grow some veg – even if the closest thing you have to a garden right now is a terrarium and one overpriced cactus.

Imported or local, pretty much all our fresh food is trucked into shops on the morning of the day it's sold

Also there's this: whether Armageddon arrives in the form of a national computer defence system becoming sentient, an airborne viral infection escaping from a laboratory or Donald Trump accidentally declaring war on the EU, one thing is certain. The UK would run out of food. Fast.

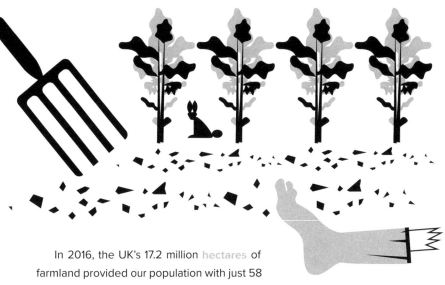

In 2016, the UK's 17.2 million hectares of farmland provided our population with just 58 per cent of all the vegetables and a mere 12 per cent of the fruit we eat.[3] We may not manage to eat our five a day, but we certainly import it. And it's not just fruit and veg: a third of all the meat we consume is imported and a quarter of the butter. Think of any food you regularly eat and chances are either it or one of its constituents has come from beyond our borders: the Netherlands, Kenya, New Zealand, the US, South America, Papua New Guinea. (Yes, we did say Papua New Guinea: it sells us about 8 per cent of our vanilla.[4] In an apocalypse, there will be no ice cream.)

Meanwhile, importers keep profits high and risks low by only holding three to four days' worth of fresh fruit and veg in their warehouses. And the wonder of modern distribution methods ensures that, whether imported or local, pretty much all our food is trucked into shops on the morning of the day it is sold. Which means that, as Ian Wright of the Food and Drink Federation told the *Guardian* in 2017, 'it only takes a break in supply... and you see those products wiped out within two or three days'.

A hectare is equivalent to 2.5 acres. That's 10,000 square metres. Or, for normal people, roughly one and a half football pitches.

Would a zombie apocalypse count as a break in supply? Was season seven of *The Walking Dead* slow-moving and repetitive compared to season one of *Black Summer*? The answer to both questions is of course yes. And when truckers don't truck, and importers can't import, we won't have long before foods start to disappear.

How long exactly?

Here's a handy table (get used to these, they're going to crop up a lot).

HANDY TABLE NO. 1 MIND THE PRODUCTION GAP

FOOD	UK PRODUCTION PER DAY	UK CONSUMPTION PER DAY	TIME UNTIL CUPBOARD IS BARE[5]
Fresh milk	6.6 million litres	13 million litres	4 days[a]
Eggs	2.8 million eggs	3.4 million eggs	4 weeks[b]
Green beans	71 tonnes	205 tonnes	4 days[c]
Apples	408 tonnes	1,224 tonnes	4 days/4 months[d]
Tomatoes	252 tonnes	1,260 tonnes	1 week/2months[e]

Wondering why apples and tomatoes have such different timescales? The UK produces roughly half the total fresh toms and a third of the apples we eat – but only in summer and autumn. The rest of the year, our cool climate means we rely on imports. If you fancy ratatouille, better hope for a June apocalypse; if you like apple crumble, pray it starts in September.

Whatever the time of year, if the majority of our farmers have joined the ranks of the undead – or, in another equally frightening scenario, no more seasonal labourers arrive from the EU – fruit, veg and cereal crops won't be harvested from the fields; they will rot where they lie. And as soon as people get a whiff of a shortage, they panic. Remember March 2012? When within just five hours of a cabinet minister saying that a tanker-driver strike *might* affect petrol supplies, fuel pumps ran dry as worried drivers poured petrol into everything from jerrycans to empty jam jars? It was chaos. Now imagine what would have happened if, while he was making that statement, the cabinet minister had been bitten by the shambling, drooling leader of the opposition. (Ed Miliband, Jeremy Corbyn – this shouldn't be hard to visualize.)

There is one supermarket in the UK for every 4,663 people in the population.[6] On any given day the average supermarket sells eight tonnes of food – enough to fill 1,500 disposable shopping bags. It will hold an average of a further eight tonnes – or twenty-four hours' worth – of food on-site. If each fear-ridden local grabs just one bag's worth of food, the shelves will be stripped bare within a day.[7] *Not so much 28 Days Later as Less Than 24 Hours Later.*

No worries, you say, supermarkets can quickly restock from their distribution centres. The trouble is supermarkets think along the same lines as importers: to maximize their profits, most only hold one day's worth of fresh food, relying on daily top-ups direct from farmers, warehouses and manufacturers. That all works OK. Until, that is, the farmers, warehouse packers and truck drivers start eating each other, and the rest of us are left pouring petrol into jam jars.

Within a matter of weeks of imports and transport failing, we'd largely be reliant on tinned food and dry goods. Of course there's nothing wrong with a diet of pasta, baked beans and rice. Ask any engineering student. Except that, without supplies of citrus fruit, tomatoes and other foods with good levels of vitamin C, it's going to be much harder to keep at bay the old curse of long-distance sailors: scurvy. Scurvy causes shortness of breath, makes your gums bleed and your teeth fall out, and stops wounds healing. It's a bit like using crystal meth, but without the insane sex drive.

What all of this adds up to is this: to survive, you're going to need your own, sustainable sources of food. That means gardening. Gardening for the zombie apocalypse.

That's where this book comes in. Zombie gardening, as we'll call it for short, doesn't mean doing some digging between slaying re-animated cadavers. Although you will of course have to slay *some* re-animated cadavers. Instead it concentrates on raising plants that provide the maximum nutrients for each square metre you grow them in. And doing it in a way that – bearing in mind society has collapsed – avoids you having to go beyond the perimeter of your fortified camp on dangerous trips to loot Londis.

This is a practical approach to gardening anyone can use, even in a small space or (boring!) if the apocalypse hasn't happened yet. Because zombie gardening is about getting maximum results while weeding out unnecessary effort, you can practise its principles in containers on a balcony, in only a small patch of soil, or even on a roof. No one is saying you need to wait for humanity to be wiped out before you grow at least some of your own food.

That word 'some' is important. Zombie gardening doesn't buy the old-fashioned myths of self-sufficiency, promulgated in the 1970s by gardeners with overlapping teeth who spent their evenings playing the flute and listening to Jethro Tull. The type of people who insist on sitting cross-legged on a perfectly usable chair. At worst, total self-sufficiency is an unachievable lie; at best, it means living like a medieval peasant, with a lot of mud, poor light levels and, yes, overlapping teeth.

Instead, zombie gardeners concentrate on growing what they can, where they can. They aren't starry-eyed about this being easy: they know from bitter experience that those TV shows where a man in a straw hat takes a dog into a vegetable garden and six weeks later harvests a hundredweight of potatoes are just lifestyle porn for people who don't know how to use the internet.

No: they understand that, as we will explain in Chapter 3, gardening is war. And in war things die. But they also know that sustainability and a healthy environment are the keys to long-term human survival. A zombie gardener would be more likely to admit there *is* a place for the flute in modern rock than to use a wide-spectrum pesticide.

Above all, zombie gardening is about growing food in a way that works. It's about knowing exactly what to do and when so that you maximize your chances of success. Before the apocalypse, if you practise zombie gardening on even the smallest scale, you won't have to make so many trips to Sainsbury's. Post the dawn of the undead, zombie gardening might just keep you alive.

So let's not waste another moment. It's time to grab that fork, meet your fellow survivors – and get gardening. ✵

SURVIVORS 'R' US

MEET YOUR ZOMBIE-GARDENING GANG

You're not going to make it on your own. Nope: you are going to have to team up with other survivors. Based on what we know from existing apocalypse stories, here's our guide to the individuals who will invariably make up your team

→

The Male Leader

He's been forced to wear a sweaty shirt and kill everyone who mattered to him. This has helped him develop astounding inner strength, outer strength and a beard.

WEAPON
Large hand gun,
shiny hatchet.

SURVIVAL POTENTIAL 9/10

The Female Leader

Pre-apocalypse, she was just an ordinary woman. Now she's a merciless, unsmiling killer who's developed astounding inner strength, outer strength and possibly a beard. Has toned upper arms and her own spin-off series.

WEAPON
Unbending determination.
And a Samurai sword.

SURVIVAL POTENTIAL 9/10

The Really Annoying Child

Plays outside the secure perimeter when told not to. Which is really annoying.

WEAPON
Doesn't matter. Whatever it is, she'll forget to bring it.

SURVIVAL POTENTIAL 1/10

The Likeable Child

Sensitive, gentle and wise beyor their years (they *never* freak out whe creeping past zombies). This mear that Likeable Child is – despite th likeability – a bit annoying.

WEAPON
Initially, a small knife.
Later, an Uzi.

The Plain Bookish Girl

Initially, a dead loss. But when the chips are down, she surprises everyone with her knowledge, resourcefulness and wry sense of humour. There is only one problem: when the zombies attack, she will lose her glasses and spend all her time on the floor looking for them.

WEAPON
Wide reading.

SURVIVAL POTENTIAL 7/10

✴✴✴✴✴✴✴✴✴✴

The Weak Academic and/or Vicar

Well-educated and therefore untrust-worthy. When being chased by a horde of the undead, he won't hold the door open long enough for you to get through.

WEAPON
None.
Will probably nick yours.

SURVIVAL POTENTIAL 2/10

✴✴✴✴✴✴✴✴✴✴

The Renegade

He has a dark past. He doesn't like to talk about it. Actually, he just doesn't like to talk. But he does have a leather waistcoat and will save the life of Really Annoying Child. Even though he shouldn't have bothered.

WEAPON
Crossbow,
his own bare hands.

SURVIVAL POTENTIAL 9/10

The Undead Beloved

Someone in your group will have at least one Undead Beloved – sometimes a child, but more often a former partner – chained up in a barn, locked in a small cupboard or tied to a post. They will escape and bite a vital team member. But on the plus side, zombie exes make good listeners.

WEAPON
Teeth.

SURVIVAL POTENTIAL 0/10*

* Duh, they're *dead*.

THE END

In *The Road*, Cormac McCarthy's sadly zombie-free but otherwise excellent post-apocalypse novel, the main character recalls how the end of the world began. He sees a strange flash of light on the horizon, then turns to his wife and says: 'Fill the bath.'

This is a good start, as apocalypses of all kinds tend to mess with water supplies. It doesn't, however, stop the man ending up pushing an empty shopping trolley through a blasted landscape towards his inevitable death.

If, on the other hand, he had gone straight out and gathered everything he needed to set up a productive vegetable garden, things might have gone better.

So what actions, other than bath-filling, should the quick-thinking prioritize on the day of

Knowing human nature, civilization's fall will come as a complete surprise. But that's OK

the undead? We're assuming, naturally, that you've not prepared in any way beforehand – to misquote Monty Python, no one expects the apocalypse, and knowing human nature, civilization's fall will come as a complete surprise. But that's OK. There are plenty of things even a completely unprepped zombie gardener can quickly do to position themselves for long-term survival. That's what we'll look at in this chapter: what to loot, save, transport and otherwise grab in those first critical, blood-spattered weeks.

PRIORITY 1
SOURCE YOUR SEEDS

At the risk of stating the bleeding obvious: plants grow from seeds. No seeds means no plants. So top of your looting list has to be these packets of DNA power.

Before the apocalypse, gardeners who wanted the widest choice of veg would order direct from seed companies. You, unfortunately, are going to have to break into the nearest garden centre. Once upon a time, you might have come here to buy Peter Rabbit table mats, scented candles or an overpriced latte. Now what you're looking for are the racks of vegetable seeds.

Packs of seed will either have use-by dates or tell you when the seed was collected. The usual rule for vegetables is that the fresher the seed, the better it will germinate, so check the pack-dates to find the freshest possible seed. But don't bother taking too much, as most commercial seed will only stay viable – which basically means 'able to germinate' – for eighteen months at the most: instead take just enough of each seed for a year's worth of planting and leave the rest for fellow survivors.

The packets you collect will be marked annual, biennial or perennial. Why is that in any way important? Because it tells you a lot about how and when your plants will crop. An annual grows, sets seed and dies in one year. In a zombie garden, that might include tomatoes, peas or runner beans. Biennials, like kale and parsley, grow only leaves in their first year, then flower, set seed and die in their second year. A perennial has top bits which die back over winter then re-sprout every spring, e.g. rhubarb or asparagus. Perennials are a bit like zombies in that you can cut

Germination is the chemical process that switches a seed on, turning it from a small, dead-looking capsule into a living entity: a bit like throwing a Poké Ball and then Jigglypuff comes out.

bits off them but they won't die; for that reason they are particularly welcome in a survival situation.

Don't bother with any annuals or biennials that are also described as 'F1 hybrid'. Pre-apocalypse, F1 varieties of veg could be very useful: they were bred by seed merchants to have particularly desirable characteristics, such as extra sweetness, size or disease resistance. But without getting too much into the fine biology, the seed they produce will not grow into a plant identical to its parent. Post-apocalypse, in a world where garden centre staff will be crashing through the Peter Rabbit table-mat display with blood dripping from their slackened jaws, you'll have to save seed from your own plants to sow the following year. We'll look at this in more detail in Chapter 4, but for now just remember that F1 annuals won't be much use to you. F1 varieties of perennials can be worth taking: F1 rhubarb seed, for instance, will, with luck, make big sturdy plants that you can crop from for years.

Perennials are a bit like zombies in that you can cut bits off them but they won't die

LOOTING LIST NO. 1

PLANTS

Amaranth

Beetroot

Broad beans

Broccoli

Cabbage

Carrots

Courgettes

French beans

Garlic

Kale

Onion

Parsnips

Peas

Potatoes

Pumpkins and squash

Runner beans

Strawberries

Swiss chard

Tomatoes

Turnips

Keep your eyes peeled for larger seed packets marked 'green manure'; these, as we will also explain in Chapter 4, are worth their weight in, well, manure, and if you use them right they will make a quantum difference to your soil.

Look out for any potted fruit trees (they'll be in the section marked 'top fruit') and pots of berry- and currant-bearing plants (in the bit marked 'soft fruit'). These are difficult to grow from seed, so you'll need to start with actual plants; loot them now, before they dry out and die from neglect.

As for which vegetables to take, grab as many different kinds as you can – the wider a selection you have, the more likely you are to grow something successfully. Having said that, we believe there are twenty key plants that best support survival in a zombie garden. You don't have to grow all of them – in fact you probably can't, as not all will suit your particular site – but just in case, here's the full looting list (left).

These key plants are so important they get their own chapter: to find out how, where and when to grow them turn to page 136.

PACK YOUR POTS

Growing food demands some specialist supplies, things like bags of seed compost and plant pots. Stocking up on these at the beginning of the apocalypse will save you having to make dangerous and time-consuming raids off-site later, particularly in the busy sowing season of February to April, when you'll need every minute to get your crops underway.

Although you can grow seeds in pretty much any container that both holds soil and allows water to drain through it, it's unlikely you'll have time to faff about Etsy-style making pots from folded newspaper, leftover egg cartons, loo rolls, yoghurt pots, etc., etc. Instead, loot a selection of ready-made containers. Easiest to use are trays of seed modules, which look like linked mini-pots; having some solid-bottomed gravel trays to stand these in makes watering and moving them much easier. See-through lids that fit over the trays will be useful for holding in humidity – a key part of getting seeds to start to grow – but aren't vital, as putting trays inside a large clear plastic bag does much the same job. And if ever you don't have a plastic bag to hand, you can always head for the nearest motorway embankment, where you'll find plenty stuck in the bushes.

As seedlings grow, you'll move them into individual pots of different sizes. Collect a range from small (3 cm) to large (12.5 cm) – square pots are better than round, because they sit nice and tight together in a tray or old vegetable crate without falling over when you're moving them round the garden.

Now head outside to where the big bags of compost are kept. Why? Well, within six months or so of starting your zombie garden, you should begin to have a supply of home-made garden compost. But this tends to be coarse, strawy and full of unwanted kinds of seeds, which will be a pain when you're sowing: you'll end up with seed trays full of different types of seedlings and won't be sure which are the ones you actually want. So take plenty of seed compost, which will be weed free, as well as lower in nutrients than ordinary all-purpose compost – overly high fertility can, oddly, stop seeds germinating.

Other than that, you'll need balls of string, for tying plants to supports. Bamboo canes of different lengths will be useful for making those supports.

> **Take plenty of seed compost, which will be weed-free and low in nutrients**

A simple soil thermometer and/or moisture probe will help you know when the ground is ready for sowing outdoors. Ready-made, all-purpose fertilizer will be a huge help until you've had time to make your own (see page 55). Blank plant labels are vital, because even without the multiple distractions of an apocalypse, no gardener in history has ever been able to remember which bloody seed they sowed where.

Then grab gardening gloves. Loads of gloves. In fact, *all* the gloves, even the pink ones with pictures of flowers printed on the back. This may seem mimsy, but being stabbed in the thumb by a thorn or a splinter when you garden is as inevitable as an alien civilization's planet-destroying weapon having an accessible weak point. We know you're

Confusingly, pot size refers to the **width at the top of the pot** rather than to how deep it is. Also, gardeners often still measure pots in inches rather than centimetres, which tells you a lot about the century they feel most comfortable in.

tough – you're surviving the end of the world, after all – but puncture wounds are the first to go septic, and in an apocalypse, there are no antibiotics.

Oh and go on, take those Peter Rabbit table mats too. You're going to need to keep warm, and they burn really well.

PRIORITY 3
TOOL UP YOUR TOOLKIT

Gardening is hard work, but the right tools will make it easier and far more productive. How big a zombie garden you have will affect which ones you prioritize. But there are some jobs that will need doing in any circumstances, so you'll need to make a swift sweep through the local hardware stores and builder's merchants. Avoid DIY superstores, though. Those shop assistants who used to stumble round the aisles like zombies? They're now zombies.

Tools for digging

One of the biggest jobs in any garden is moving soil around. So you'll need a fork and/or a spade to remove deep-rooted weeds and big stones, and to harvest many crops, plus a trowel for making holes for young plants and a small hand fork for digging at close quarters. If you only have room for either a fork or a spade, take the fork: the prongs mean it exerts more pressure on a smaller area and so is more efficient.

Rakes are also vital for getting your soil ready for sowing. A seed rake (the kind with a flat, oblong head and widely spaced teeth) is best for breaking soil into the much finer particles you need

for a seed bed. If you have room, add a drag rake – three big, curved prongs on the end of a long handle – as it's great for breaking up big clods.

If you actively enjoy grubbing around with your face five inches from the earth, you can weed with a hand fork. But a sharp-edged, long-handled hoe is the quicker, not-mental option. Small-headed draw hoes are good for dragging across the surface of the soil between narrow rows of veg, but the wider push-and-pull kind, which cut weeds down just below the surface, are quicker at covering large spaces.

Don't bother looting powered

digging tools such as rotavators. Their blades only work the top few inches of the soil, leaving the deeper layers untouched; they can't cope with long grass, big stones, or very heavy or wet soils; and they will slice the roots of perennial weeds such as creeping thistle and dock into lots of tiny pieces. That's absolutely the worst thing to do to a plant able to regenerate an entire new body from a single shred. Think of the thing that eats Jake Gyllenhaal in the film *Life* – that's exactly how a couple of centimetres of dock root will behave given half a chance. Also once fuel supplies run out, your rotavator will sit around uselessly taking up space. Again like Jake Gyllenhaal in *Life*.

These machines are so noisy they'd attract any zombie within 500 metres. So we'd say leave them behind

Tools for cutting

A zombie garden needs some tools for small-scale cutting and some for large.

Bypass secateurs, the kind where the top blade slices past the bottom blade, will be useful for pruning any fruit brushes you grow, as well as for harvesting medium- to thin-stemmed crops like sprouting broccoli or French beans. A fixed-blade gardener's knife would be useful for harvesting thicker-stemmed crops such as sweetcorn or pumpkins, but there's no reason you can't use a sturdy kitchen knife instead.

You'll also need tools for cutting down standing plants. A brush hook looks like a medieval bill, which was designed for taking down knights in armour – for bigger gardens, it'll be just as useful for slashing large areas of green manure, nettles or bracken. For small sites, a good pair of shears can do much the same job. Plus you're less likely to take your own leg off.

As with digging tools, there are plenty of powered cutters around: strimmers, shredders, rotary lawn mowers... But as we'll see, the supplies of petrol, diesel and electricity you need to run them are all going to be problematic. And anyway, these machines are so noisy they'd attract any zombie within 500 metres. So we'd say leave them behind.

Tools for watering

Unless the apocalypse is the *Blade Runner* kind and it never stops raining, you'll need help irrigating your plants. So grab a couple of ten-litre watering cans, along with one of the normal pierced heads known as 'roses' and one of the extra-fine kind. A small can with an ultra-fine rose will be helpful for watering delicate seedlings without knocking them flat.

A hosepipe is an essential time saver in any size of garden – best is the slightly heavier, double-walled kind that doesn't kink too easily. For larger spaces, seep hoses, made of semi-rigid plastic with regular holes along their length, lie directly on the earth and slowly drip out water; teamed with a timer on a tap or pump, they can water entire beds while you're busy with other jobs.

Plastic butts that collect rainwater from gutter downpipes can be linked together to collect as much water as possible from roofs. But consider using old household cold-water tanks instead, as you can save fill-time by dipping watering cans directly into them. In an emergency, you can also push zombies in them, as they find the steep sides difficult to climb.

Tools for wood

The arrival of the apocalypse means you'll become increasingly familiar with chopping things up. Not just zombies, but wood. Yes, it can help with heating and cooking, but you're also going to need timber for building and repairing garden infrastructure. That means gathering a selection of axes: a 4.5 lb. version, a heavy 6.5 or 8 lb. splitting maul for splitting logs into halves and quarters, and a light hatchet for chopping up smaller logs without wearing yourself out.

You'll need saws, too: a curved bowsaw is easiest for cutting trunks into manageable sections, while a straight wood saw will be more use when you're cutting planks.

This is the point where you might be tempted by a chainsaw. The trouble is they're lethal. All the manuals say they're so dangerous that you should only use them while wearing special

You'll become increasingly familiar with chopping things up. Not just zombies, but wood

trousers, special boots, special gloves and a special helmet. This, in an apocalypse, is asking a bit much. Also, you should never hold a chainsaw above head height, even when undertaking massacres in Texas for cannibalistic purposes : Leatherface, please note, this is for your own safety. And if you bury the wrong part of the blade – the top edge of the tip – into either a zombie or a tree, the saw will kick back and bury itself in you instead. So while they are brilliant at getting through large trunks and chunks of firewood, we'd say stick to hand tools.

Before you leave, pile all your lootings into a wheelbarrow: any plot larger than a patio will need one for moving compost, collecting harvests and transporting young plants. Most wheelbarrows have pneumatic tyres, but these have a habit of bursting and/or puncturing. The old-fashioned kind with solid wheels may be bumpier when you're pushing them around, but you'll never have to waste time changing the tyre or mending a puncture.

LOOTING LIST NO. 3
GARDEN TOOLS

Fork
Spade
Hand fork
Trowel
Long-handled hoe
Rake
Bypass secateurs
Brush hook or shears
Hosepipe
Watering cans, plus roses
Selection of axes and saws
Wheelbarrow

PRIORITY 4
FILL YOUR CUPBOARDS (BUT NOT YOUR FRIDGE)

Yes, we know this book is about how to grow your own food. But nature can't be rushed. Even if the zombie apocalypse is helpful enough to start in early spring, which for most temperate-grown crops is the beginning of the sowing season, plants grow slowly: it will be months before you're able to harvest anything worth eating.

Mains-powered refrigeration will no longer be a reliable means of storing food

In medieval times, May was known as 'the hungry month', because by then everyone had exhausted their winter stores but even the earliest of the new season's crops were still weeks away. And if the apocalypse starts in early autumn, you're looking at a nine-month wait before you can start to eat your own produce.

Short on power

The zombie gardener's (i.e. your) response to this is probably to run out of the house with your new wheelbarrow and raid the local Aldi. Good plan. Except as we showed in the introduction: it won't be long until Aldi is Empti. And though you might fill your trolleys with meat and twenty-two veg, fresh food, even when refrigerated, doesn't last that long. As for refrigeration itself – well...

- There are 285 power plants operated by the major producers in the UK, with a combined potential output of 74,373 megawatts.[8]
- Coal-, gas- and oil-fired plants provide 60 per cent of this output; without refuelling or maintenance they'd be likely to stop working within twelve to thirty-six hours.
- Hydroelectric-, solar- and wind-power stations provide 16 per cent. These don't need refuelling but do need humans to maintain them; without intervention they'd be likely to begin failing after a few weeks.
- Nuclear plants provide 12 per cent of our electricity (the remaining percentage is produced by outliers: straw-powered plants or ones that are fuelled by meat) and have enough stores to last about a year without refuelling. But if enough of their operators fail to turn up to work – or turn up with a new appetite for snacking on other people's brains – their safety systems should shut them down after approximately a week. And if they don't? Put it like this: you're unlikely to survive the zombie apocalypse by moving to Hinkley.

Once power stations start going offline, you get an imbalance between power generation and demand. And once the number of non-zombified employees available to manage this imbalance across the grid drops significantly, power cuts and blackouts will be unavoidable, and mains-powered refrigeration will no longer be a reliable means of storing food.

Yes, there is a meat-fuelled power station. **We know: ewww. But in an apocalypse, anything that could in theory convert zombies into electricity will be totally welcome.**

Strong and staple

Without refrigeration, you might as well leave that pack of sausages in the chiller cabinet and concentrate instead on looting enough dry goods and store-cupboard staples to keep you going for the worst-case scenario of nine months before your first harvest.

Rice and pasta will provide plenty of carbs, but flour contains more calories by volume and weight, so if your storage space is limited, make for the baking goods. (Which also means that – hooray – slobbing out in front of *Bake Off* counts as legitimate preparation for the apocalypse!) And don't forget you'll need protein for muscle mass – no one without biceps can stab a zombie in the eye or push a wheelbarrow up a hill. Peanuts, almonds, walnuts, hazelnuts and lentils all pack in a lot of protein (and calories) for their weight. As for vitamin C, weight for weight, dried lychees are the kings, containing 168 mg of vitamin per 100 g of lychee. Time to put the local Chinese supermarket on your loot route.

Next, look for packets of fortified (as opposed to natural) brewer's yeast, the kind that can be used for making alcohol and bread. Not because eating toast and getting pissed will make the apocalypse more bearable – though it will – but because it contains vitamin B12. Nuts, cereals and several zombie-garden

veg are sources of most B vitamins, but unless your site has room for egg-, milk- or meat-producing animals, B12 will be in short supply.

And now we come to preservation. Without reliable refrigeration, you'll need to use a lot of old-fashioned methods of extending the edible life of your crops outside the growing season. We'll come back to this in Chapter 6, but for now, you need to make sure you have supplies of the basics for preserving: vinegar, salt, oil and sugar. Of these, salt – unless you live by the sea – is going to be the one that you will find hardest to supplement yourself in the post-zombie future, so make sure you stock up with plenty. For everything else, the amounts we've suggested on the right should be enough to feed one adult survivor for one post-apocalypse month.

And so it begins

There you have it. The first weeks of the apocalypse are drawing to a close. Most of the population is dead, and semi-decomposed brain-biters lurk around every corner. You, however, are ready to make a start on surviving, with cupboards full of basic foodstuffs and a shedful of tools, plants and seed.

But there is one last thing you need. A site. Where to find it, and what it should look like, we'll discuss in the next chapter. Meantime, you need to get a vehicle and get moving. ✳

We've given amounts for one adult because children would skew the figures. Plus they refuse to eat veg anyway.

LOOTING LIST NO. 4
FOOD

1.5kg	**Pasta**
1.5kg	**Rice**
3kg	**Oats**
3kg	**Dried lentils**
3kg	**Dried kidney beans**
1.3kg	**Wholewheat flour**
1kg	**Peanut butter**
0.84kg	**Walnuts/Hazelnuts**
0.40kg	**Vegetable oil**
0.90kg	**Dried lychees**

Plus as much as you can carry of salt, sugar, spirit vinegar and fortified brewer's yeast.

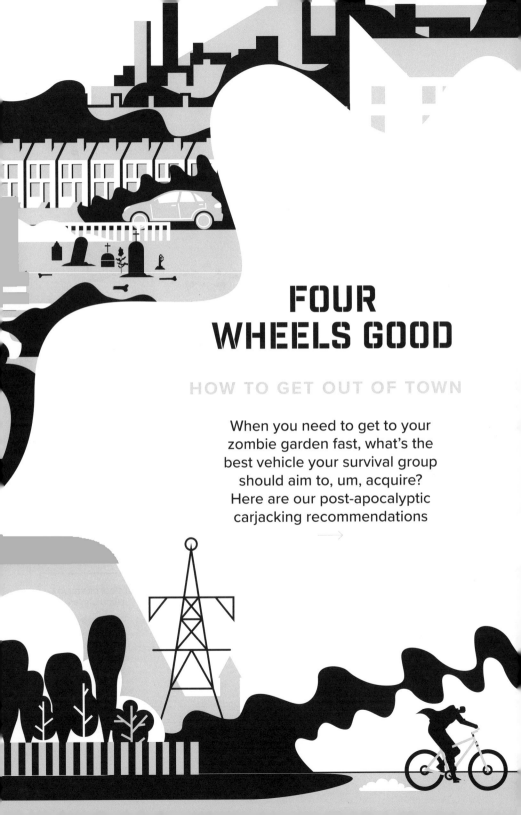

FOUR
WHEELS GOOD

HOW TO GET OUT OF TOWN

When you need to get to your zombie garden fast, what's the best vehicle your survival group should aim to, um, acquire? Here are our post-apocalyptic carjacking recommendations

The reliable small car

Nobody wants to break down in an apocalypse. That probably means nicking a car made by a Japanese manufacturer, whose models regularly top the reliability tables. Plus a shortage of working petrol stations means that a fuel-efficient one-litre hatchback would be handy. But any survivor sitting in the back will have got cramp before you're twenty miles out.

The large-scale motorhome

Unlike a hatchback, this will have all the space you need for packing in the whole of your group, plus their supplies. But we wouldn't recommend going on holiday in a motorhome, so why would you spend the apocalypse in one?

No car

The safest bet of all may be a bicycle. When everyone flees at the same time, huge, zombie-attracting traffic jams are inevitable. A bike, though, is quiet and fuel free and allows you to nip off-road to your zombie garden.

The luxury four-by-four

You know the sort of thing we mean: climbs vertical slopes, guzzles petrol and drops off small children at preschool. Unlike the motorhome, these babies have the horsepower to get you out of a hole fast – and in an apocalypse, who cares about particulates?

Your own car

When was the last time you broke into a modern car, bypassed the wheel lock and jump-started the ignition? Unless you are an expert thief, the best car for the zombie apocalypse is the car you've got the keys for.

Just don't wear skin-tight Lycra while you're cycling, as it provides no protection against zombie bites. And it'll look like you're having a mid-life crisis. In an apocalypse.

PEPPER IN A POT

The apocalypse hasn't started yet, you're stuck in a flat-share above Chicken Cottage and the council has sold off all the local allotments to property developers with no interest in the phrase 'affordable housing'. Don't worry! You can still zombie-garden. It might be on a smaller scale than your ideal post-apocalypse set-up, but growing even a fraction of your own food now will develop crucial skills, skills that will keep you alive after the arrival of the undead.

Does your home have an area out back for the rubbish? Or a flat roof, with some way of getting up to it? Does it have a sunny windowsill? Or any kind of balcony? That's your zombie garden right there. Because as long as you give it enough light, moisture, food and soil, pretty much any plant will grow in a container – and that includes cropping plants. With a bit of care and attention, you can zombie-garden herbs in small pots on a windowsill, and lettuces, tomatoes and carrots in bigger pots on a balcony.

But how about something a little more unusual? Something that, come the apocalypse and the end of imports, you won't be able to get your hands on? Like, say, pepper.

The Szechuan pepper bush (known to non-zombie gardeners by its Latin name, *Zanthoxylum schinifolium*) is a tough, spiny shrub that will grow well despite dry, windy or cold conditions. That makes it a good contender for an exposed roof, a sun-blasted balcony, or that bit by the bins where the scary neighbour's Staffie always pees. And its crop – pinkish peppercorns that you harvest in autumn – can be ground and used solo as an alternative to black pepper or as part of a classic Chinese five-spice mix.

So yes, you may be stuck in a flat-share above Chicken Cottage. But a) they give you a discount on Monday nights, and b) you can always spice up your BBQ Bonanza box with a grind of zombie-gardened pink pepper. Here's how.

1 SOURCE YOUR PLANT

Szechuan pepper is not (yet) a garden-centre standard, so look online for specialist nurseries and plant suppliers, many of which do mail order. Aim to buy one that comes in a 2.5-litre or 5-litre pot, as anything smaller will need two or three years of nursing before it's big enough to fruit.

2 GIVE IT A DRINK

When it arrives, unpack it straight away and plunge it into a sink or bucket of water until any bubbles of air stop rising. Then remove it and let the excess water drain out.

3 CHOOSE A CONTAINER

Now choose your container. You can use anything from a traditional terracotta pot to an old wastepaper bin to plant into – just make sure you make some holes in the bottom for water to drain through. The container shouldn't be much more than about five centimetres larger across the top than the pot the plant came in; otherwise, the excess soil around the edges can get too wet and rot the roots.

4 CHOOSE YOUR COMPOST

As this is a plant that can grow up to three or four metres high and wide, you need to use something called soil-based compost to give your container weight and hold it steady. Any bag of compost with the tag 'John Innes No. 3' will have the right kind of mix. Or you can make your own: a 3:2:1 mix of topsoil, garden compost and the kind of washed, large-grained (aka sharp) sand you find at garden centres.

7 POT IT UP

Add a layer of compost to the bottom of your new container, then put the pepper plant on top of it and fill the gaps around the edges with more compost. Don't let the compost go higher than the top of the plant's existing soil, as that might rot the stem. But try to sit the whole thing several centimetres below the rim of your container, as that will make watering a much quicker business.

5 GIVE IT A KNOCK

Get the plant out by banging the pot on its bottom. Don't yank the plant by the stem, as that's a bit like grabbing a zombie by the neck: its head will likely come right off. Though in an undead-attack situation that's a good thing, in a trying-to-grow-something situation it's less of a positive.

6 FREE ITS ROOTS

If the roots look what's known as pot-bound — growing in a tight circle round themselves, or so densely matted that you can hardly see any earth — dig your fingers into the root ball and open it up a bit. Use a knife if you need, and don't worry too much about breaking a few bits of root, as that will encourage new ones to grow.

8 GIVE IT ANOTHER DRINK

While we're on the subject: water straight away, until you see liquid running out of the bottom of the pot. Then keep the plant out of direct sun for the first few days, to help it cope with what's known as transplant shock. During the growing season — when the bush has green leaves on it — water the pot right through whenever the soil feels dry 2.5 cm or more below the surface.

> Relax: we're not going to make a bad joke about gender identity. All transplant means is moving a plant to a new home.

9 KEEP IT FED

From late spring until the first flowers appear, feed about once a week with a liquid fertilizer: look for the kinds marked 'all-purpose'. Also, follow the dilution instructions on the bottle, as although plants can neither develop type-two diabetes nor take up more than one seat on the bus, overfeeding is still bad for them.

10 GET PICKING

By late summer you'll be able to see any fruits that are going to form. (Be patient: you may not get any flowers or fruit for the first year or two as, like people, shrubs need to grow up a bit before they can get into the whole reproduction thing.) Once the papery outsides of these fruits start peeling and splitting, they're ripe, and the pepper seed, or corn, is ready to collect. Pick the corns off the plant, leave to dry in a warm, airy place, then pull off any stalks and put what's left – skins and all – into your pepper mill. You can freeze any spare peppercorns for up to a year before they'll start to lose their flavour.

11 KEEP IT GOING

Szechuan pepper bushes are one of those excellent plants that can keep on cropping year after year. But to keep them going, watch for the leaves to drop in autumn, then only water if the pot is about to dry out completely. Also watch the weather forecasts: to stop the roots freezing solid and dying, swaddle the pot in bubble wrap if the temperature is due to go much below -2° C. In spring, move your plant, root ball and all, into a new and slightly bigger container, and start watering/feeding again. Do this every other year until your plant has reached its full size; after that, you can kick back and just refresh the top third of the soil rather than repotting the whole lot.

And if the scary neighbour's Staffie pees on it every now and again, well, yay: urine has nitrogen in it and nitrogen makes plants grow. As you'll find out when you get to Chapter 4. But first, let us introduce you to Chapter 2. ✳

THE PLOT THICKENS

You can't garden without a garden to garden in.
Or can you?

There's an old English saying: 'A man with five acres and a cow is a rich man indeed.' In other words, at a time when farmers farmed without mechanization or industrially produced inorganic fertilizers, five acres of good soil, plus an animal to milk, would provide the average family with all their own needs. Plus it would give them plenty of surplus grain, veg, meat and milk to sell to and/or barter with their wider community. In an ideal apocalypse – and yes, we know that's a dumb phrase – every zombie gardener and their band of fellow survivors would scour the countryside until they found themselves five acres of land.

Initially, of course, that might not be possible. Some zombie gardeners might be trapped in cities by impassable hordes of shambling corpses. Others might not have suitable transport to get out into the country and on to high-quality, fertile farmland. They might have to make the best of their

> Some of you might have to make the best of your immediate surroundings for a year or two

immediate surroundings for a year or two before they can strike out into the depopulated countryside. And even those who do make it to rural paradise might not have the manpower to adequately patrol the 1,000 m of boundary (roughly two and a half times a standard athletics track) that surrounds a five-acre plot.

So in this chapter we'll look at some of the alternatives. In town or out of it, we'll show you how to judge the strengths, weaknesses and food-growing potential of any likely zombie-garden site, from patio size all the way up to football pitch.

NEED NO. 1
SPACE

The ideal zombie garden would be big enough to grow sufficient food to keep you and your group of survivors alive. But how big is that? The past provides at least a partial answer.

From the eighteenth century on, various charitable enterprises and acts of parliament tried to encourage land owners to allot food-growing space to the poor. But these 'allotment gardens' only really took off during the First World War, when German naval blockades made importing so risky that Britain – which, in a familiar tale, didn't grow enough to feed itself – was in danger of starving. In February 1917 the prime minister at the time, David Lloyd George, passed the Cultivation of Lands Order,[9] leading to the creation of huge numbers of allotments. The belief was that ten rods – or 250 square metres – of garden was enough to keep you away from the greengrocer's and 'ensure a sufficiency of supplies for an average family all year round... except where grown-up sons and daughters with particularly healthy appetites have to be fed'.[10]

So, as long as they've got rid of any boomeranging twenty-somethings, a family with two children can support itself on 250 square metres. Which means the minimum amount of space you'd need to keep one adult apocalypse survivor alive and healthy is around eighty square metres.

That doesn't allow for grain production, though. You'll likely want to grow some kind of cereal — oats, wheat, barley, quinoa (no, we're not joking) — as a staple. Livestock like sheep or cows will give you useful B vitamins in meat or milk. An orchard or, better, a forest garden — a largely self-fertilizing mix of fruit trees, nut trees and cropping shrubs — would provide you with extra vitamin C and protein. And then there's fuel: the perfect zombie garden would be surrounded by coppiced woodland, for keeping your house warm with a post-apocalypse wood-burning Aga.

In other words, what you're really looking for is a secure house with a big vegetable patch, an area twice as big again for cereals, a couple of fields of pasture for grazing, an established orchard and easy access to existing woodland. Plus animal shelters, hay barns, several large sheds and a lovely big zombie-proof wall all the way around it.

Unfortunately, most of us won't be able to secure a farm from an Edwardian children's novel. We will have to look elsewhere.

Unfortunately, most of us won't be able to secure a farm from an Edwardian children's novel. We will have to look elsewhere

Space to grow

Where exactly should you look? Well, in an apocalypse, any amount of food is a bonus. So the wise zombie gardener will consider what space is closest to hand and then work out how much they could grow there. For example:

- **Balconies** In new two-bed London flats, typical planning laws will state that any balconies have to be at least six square metres.[11] Cover one of these with growbags and that's enough space to grow fifteen tomato plants, giving you up to 58 kg of toms – the equivalent of thirty-odd 500 ml bottles of passata.[12]
- **Back gardens** In 2014, the average British back garden was thirteen square metres.[13] That may seem pretty small, but it's still enough space to grow 8.6 kg of wheat – or enough flour to make seventeen large wholemeal loaves.[14]
- **Communal gardens** Developers including a communal garden with an apartment block typically have to allow for fifteen square metres of garden per unit.[15] That means a block of ten new-build flats would have enough outside space to grow 52 kg of dried French beans in a year – the equivalent of 125 standard tins of Heinz baked beans.

This amount of wheat is based on how much British farmers produce from a hectare, by the way. But less 20 per cent. Why? Because farmers are a) experts and b) able to use chemical fertilizers, herbicides and/or pesticides – which, after the first few months of an apocalypse, survivors won't have easy access to. Unless they've locked themselves inside the perimeter of a chemical fertilizer, herbicide and/or pesticide factory. Which would be odd.

NEED NO. 2
SOIL

The success of any zombie garden is built literally from the ground up: your garden will only ever be as good as the soil you grow it in. Soil is what holds your crops in position, what feeds and waters them. It doesn't come in just one variety, either. The kind of soil you have will make all the difference to what kind of food you can grow and how successfully, so you should take time to assess what kind you have.

Sites with earth

In gardens and open spaces like allotments, check your soil by doing what's called a pit test. Once you've picked a likely spot, take a spade and begin digging a squarish hole in the ground.

To start with, the soil will be reasonably dark: this is the living, nutrient-rich layer known as topsoil, where plant roots will be happiest. As you dig deeper, the soil will change colour, usually getting much lighter. This is subsoil, which isn't nearly so root friendly. With less than 15 cm of topsoil, growing any food crop other than shallow-rooters like herbs or lettuce won't be easy, so look elsewhere.

If you've been sensible and looted either a battery-powered soil probe or a soil-testing kit, use it to check the soil pH, i.e. how acid or alkaline it is. If your probe shows 'pH 7', the soil is neutral; above 7 is alkaline; below is acid. Most zombie-garden plants will grow happily in soil with a pH between 6.5 and 7.5. But poorly drained, very acidic earth – the kind with a pH of 5.0 or lower – won't support the kinds of plants a zombie gardener needs to survive. Again, look elsewhere.

Next, moisten the soil in your hand and see if it will roll into a ball that holds its shape when you drop it. If it basically behaves like Plasticine, the soil is clay. This is made of tiny mineral particles that cling together in sheets; it holds nutrients well but will get wet in winter and dry to rock hard in summer.

If the soil won't roll into a ball at all, it's sandy: made of larger mineral particles with lots of air space between them. This means that water drains through it very fast, and keeping your crops watered and fed will take more time and energy – time and energy that after the dawn of the dead would be more usefully spent:

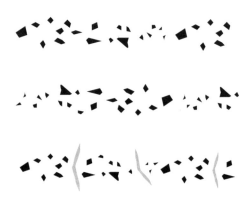

- Patrolling boundaries and doing martial-arts training with a sharp stick.
- Growing closer as a community by sharing stories about your lives before the apocalypse.
- Raiding other settlements and facing heavy moral decisions about whether to kill all the occupants. Then killing all the occupants, with sharp sticks.

If the soil ball holds its shape until you drop it and then breaks, it is garden manna: loam, a light, rich, friendly mixture of mineral particles large and small, which you can plant in all seasons and which doesn't dry out too quickly.

A last note: according to Cranfield University's brilliantly useful soil-mapping Land Information System, the

The word minerals has two meanings for zombie gardeners: either the ground-down particles of rock that, in different sizes, make up the basis of soil, or chemicals such as iron and magnesium that plants need for healthy growth.

area around the nuclear plant at Hinkley Point is made of loamy sand, with a peaty surface, high groundwater and a medium to high carbon content [16]. This means it is really fertile. Still: don't go there.

Sites with no earth

On balconies, roofs, prison yards or any place where growing has to happen in containers, you'll need to source some kind of growing medium. The good news is this means you can control its quality; the bad news is you have to loot great big heavy bags of compost.

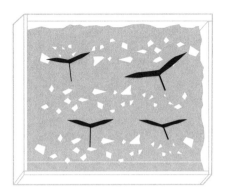

For successful vegetable harvests, you'll need your growing medium to be airy, able to drain well, and to contain plenty of a vital ingredient known as 'organic matter' (OM). This is a rotted mix of dead plants and animal matter – straw, dung, fallen leaves, zombie flesh – that helps hold water, feed soil microorganisms and provide plant nutrients. Multipurpose compost will be the right texture and have a high proportion of OM; you'll find it in just-about-luggable twenty-five-litre bags at garden centres and DIY stores. Green-waste compost, the kind piled up in bags for pre-apocalypse sale at council rubbish and recycling centres, can be a bit more hit and miss, quality-wise, but is still worth grabbing. You might also come across pure bagged topsoil, though this is unlikely to have much OM and is really heavy: don't try to loot it on your own.

How many bags will you need? You might be surprised by the sums. One piddly container 30 cm wide and 30 cm deep will swallow up the entire contents of a twenty-five-litre bag of compost. For a single square metre of raised bed 25 cm deep, you'll need to carry home a hefty ten bags. But look at it this way: by the end of the apocalypse you'll be really ripped.

A raised bed can be one of two things. The first is just an area of earth that's been mounded up a few centimetres above soil level so that it warms up more quickly in spring. The second is used on soil-less sites: it's a kind of large box built of brick or wood and filled with compost – plus a lot of cats who can't believe what a brilliant toilet you've just made them.

NEED NO. 3
SUN

You, us and everything else moving about on this planet gets its nutrition by chowing down on living organisms. Whales eat krill, humans eat avocado on toast, zombies eat brains. The one amazing exception is plants. They make their own food, using just carbon dioxide – the stuff we have to get rid of – water and light. This makes plants both jaw-droppingly clever and actual breatharians.

Some types of plant are naturally slow growers, so they don't need high light levels – think of woodland ferns or ivy. But most food plants are either heavy croppers or fast growers, and that means they need a lot of sunshine. There really is no point trying to grow peas in the deep shade thrown by a wall or a tree. As a plant that germinates, shoots several feet into the air, bears heavy loads of sugar-rich seeds and then dies, all in the space of a year, they simply won't get access to enough light energy to do their thing.

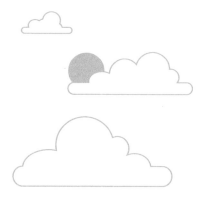

So for a maximum harvest, your main growing area should be open ground that gets the sun, without any areas of shade, for as long as possible. As the sun travels across the sky from east to west, south-facing sites get the least shade, north-facing sites the most. If you're growing in an area that is lightly shaded for part of the day, growth will be slightly reduced; if it's deeply shaded for the majority of the day, look for a different site. And if you're growing on a balcony, be aware that plants at the back will get a lot less sun than the front.

NEED NO. 4
WATER

Vegetable plants are thirsty creatures. Rainfall will provide some of their needs, but to guarantee good crops they need a steadier, more controllable supply than the weather alone can usually manage. That means your zombie garden should have its own back-up source of irrigation.

The rules are the same for any site. Whether you're growing on a roof or a smallholding, the source should be as close as possible to your growing area to save both time and energy. Ideally it should also be slightly above your growing area. That way you can use gravity – rather than electricity or muscle-power – to move the water around.

In the countryside, your source could be a spring, a well, a pond or a stream, although ground immediately next to rivers is best avoided, as it's likely to flood in winter. In towns and cities it's most likely you'll be relying on the rainwater you can collect in butts and tanks. Before the apocalypse we had taps, of course, but mains water pressure will drop as soon as the pumping stations fail. And anyway, plants seem to grow better on rainwater than tap water: it's pretty much pure H_2O, with no fluoride or leached minerals to upset the little green fusspots.

NEED NO. 5
SHELTER

You think a zombie apocalypse makes gardening difficult? Try growing anything in strong winds. Wind slows a plant down, because to survive it has to divert energy from making fruit or new, soft green growth (the bits we tend to eat) and instead reinforce its stems with a woody, strengthening substance called lignin. Wind also sucks water from plants' tissues; it carries spores of fungal diseases; and if that's not enough, it can knock crops flat on their backs. Usually just when you're about to harvest them.

Across the UK the wind blows most often from the south-west, so don't choose an exposed site by the sea in the West Country. (Hinkley, anyone?) Cold north-easterlies flatten, freeze and otherwise, um, shock and awe winter crops, which means high ground in Scotland or Northumberland is also not what you'd call a top choice. And if you're forced to survive in towns and cities, gardens on roofs will be blasted by wind from all sides.

There are some ways to reduce wind's impact. Trees and hedges around the edges of large sites, or tall crops like Jerusalem artichokes or bamboo on the borders of small sites, all create wind-filtering shelter belts. Any buildings around or above your site will have some slowing effect. And a site a third of the way down a slope will be partly protected from wind by the ground above.

Avoid sites right at the bottom of hills, though. They're often what's known as frost pockets, where the coldest, heaviest air hangs about all winter long. This is great if you fancy re-creating an episode of *Dancing on Ice*, but it's no help for a garden.

NEED NO. 6
FERTILITY

We've already established that plants make their own magic food from sunlight. Hooray! Except they don't. They also need to absorb a whole load of chemical nutrients from the soil. And heavy-cropping vegetable plants are particularly hungry: if you grow them in the same place year after year, they can quickly drain soil of its fertility.

This means you have to work hard to maintain and, if possible, improve nutrient levels. To start with, looted chemical fertilizers can do the job, but in the long term you'll need to look at more sustainable methods.

Ideally, you'd create something called a closed-loop garden, where all the nutrients that your plants use up are continuously replaced by resources that come from your own site. This is about as achievable as a perpetual-motion machine, but there's no harm in aiming to create, say, an almost-closed loop. (A 'loo'?) We'll look at how to do this in more detail in Chapter 4, but for now just be aware you've got three main nutrient-boosting options:

- Recycling food and garden waste to make compost
- Keeping animals to provide manure
- Growing the kinds of plants that add nutrients to soil, aka green manures

Ideally you'll use a combination of all three methods – but that of course depends on your site. Which brings us to the next need: good planning.

ORGANIZATION

Any zombie-garden site of any size needs a ground plan. If you just dive in and start digging without considering your plants' needs, you won't get the maximum nutritional return on the energy you spend growing them.

So like all good generals, before you start, look at your resources and draw up a list of achievable aims. Where will your plants get the most light? Which spots have the easiest access to water? How much shelter will you need to build, or plant, to protect your crops? And most vital of all: which plants will grow best in the kind of soil you've got? (If that last bit's got you worried, Chapter 5 can help.)

To show you what we mean, here are sample layouts for three absolutely real and believable zombie gardens.

Alan Titchmarsh, **MBE**, is a gardener, television presenter and also novelist. His third novel, *Mr Macgregor* (Simon & Schuster, 2004), is about a sexually magnetic TV gardener. The question most frequently asked of Alan is 'Where do you get your ideas from?'

Plan A: The 1990s-housing-development back garden

Before the apocalypse, this suburban back garden was half lawn. The other half was covered in decking, which was both a waste of valuable growing space and unpleasantly reminiscent of an Alan Titchmarsh makeover show.

Post-apocalypse, the zombie gardener has ripped up the decking while shouting 'Oy, Titchmarsh — decking is what you stand on when you're on a boat!' and dug up the lawn to create a vegetable bed. This is centrally sited to keep it away from shade cast by the fencing and edged with some of the decking planks.

The rest of the decking and a couple of old window frames now make up two shallow wooden boxes with glass lids, facing north-east and north-west to keep them out of too much direct sunlight. Called 'cold frames', these are ideal places to shelter very young

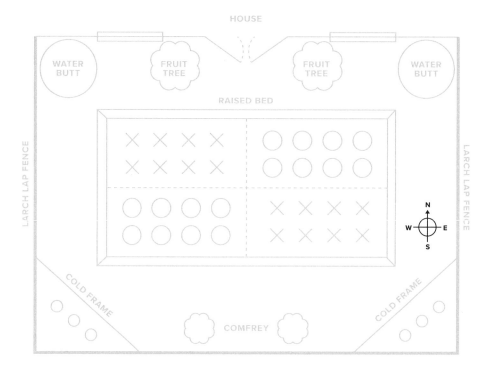

PLAN A BACK GARDEN

plants, after they've germinated on the south-facing kitchen window and before they're ready to go into the raised bed.

Irrigation comes from two water butts fed by guttering from the house roof.

Two pot-grown patio fruit trees benefit from the maximum light and warmth of the south-facing wall.

As there is no space for compost-making, this zombie garden relies on green manure: a perennial called comfrey (see page 117) in deep pots, and annual red clover and ryegrass sown in the bed between crops.

Because the vegetable bed is relatively small, this zombie gardener has wisely decided to maximize its value by concentrating on plants that don't need long growing seasons before they crop. And they have mixed vertical plants with low spreading growers to eke out each centimetre of space. A mix of tomatoes, Swiss chard, turnips, runner beans and savoy cabbage will provide them with vitamin C across two seasons, greens for nine months of the year, and – if they dry the beans – carbohydrates in winter.

Plan B: The architecturally important tower-block roof

The flat roof of this hideous but listed 1960s landmark provides a lot of potential growing space. Unfortunately the local soil is a heavy clay and has to be transported up all sixteen storeys; that's hard work, and in an apocalypse the lifts won't be working. (Though actually, they didn't work before. Which the estate agent who let the place out forgot to mention.) So while this site holds a total of eighty square metres of raised beds – enough to provide a year's calories for one survivor – they're kept relatively shallow, at 22 cm deep, to reduce the amount of soil. This also means the roof is less likely to collapse: in or out of an apocalypse, that's always a plus.

Because the beds are on a hard surface, plants can't access water from any soil beneath and in dry weather will need lots of irrigation. As there are no pitched roofs to hand (Brutalists didn't do slanting), the gardener has built a double-faced water catcher instead. Made from lightweight corrugated roofing sheets fixed at a sixty-degree pitch to a wooden frame, this channels rainwater via a series of raised, linked water butts to the growing area.

Closed beds like these are easily exhausted by both heavy cropping and water washing away nutrients. Luckily there's room here for a series of large compost heaps, where all the garden waste gets recycled before going back onto the beds. And chicken poo from the coop gives the soil a boost at planting-out time.

Against the south-facing wall of the stairwell, the survivor has used window frames looted from the flats below to build a simple, lean-to greenhouse. Because it has three glass walls as well as a glass roof, this is much warmer than a cold frame, and is useful for germinating and protecting seedlings as well as growing veg.

Up high like this, wind is a major problem. Bamboo planted around the outside edges of the roof, in galvanized-steel water tanks from abandoned flats filters out some of the wind and provides edible shoots in spring.

The raised beds are filled with low-growing plants that can cope with heavy soils: things like dwarf French beans, squash, turnips, ballhead cabbage and strawberries. Growing in the greenhouse

PLAN B ROOFTOP GARDEN

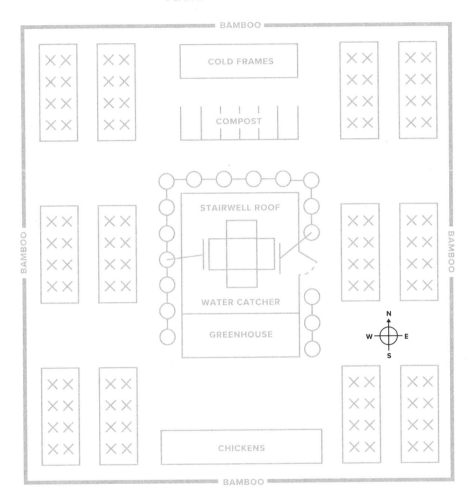

are indoor varieties of tomatoes, early crops of broad beans and winter crops of leaf beet. It also provides a home for winter potatoes, planted in August in compost-filled dustbins – there are no rubbish collections in the apocalypse – and ready to harvest anytime between late December and April. If this doesn't work, the bins will make effective aerial bombs for dropping on the zombie horde below. Or on the estate agent who didn't mention the lifts.

Plan C: The Premier League football stadium

At 1.7 acres (that's 7,000 square metres) the pitch of this all-grass football stadium makes a seriously big zombie garden.

And it is a great spot for seeing out the apocalypse – there's good all-round light, the cantilevered seating means the growing area is sheltered from the wind, and the layout has been planned so that the site can now fully support up to eight

PLAN C STADIUM GARDEN

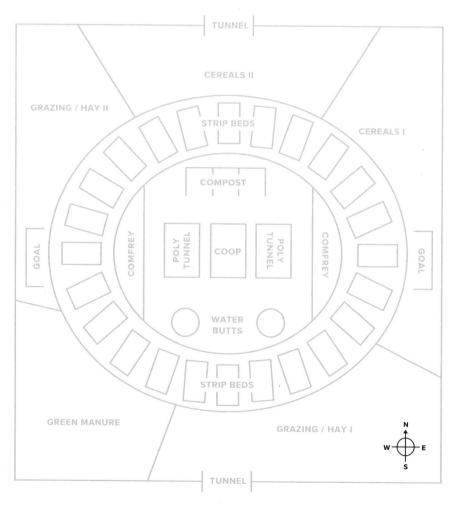

survivors. Plus the club shop is a useful source of free activewear.

Compost heaps, water tanks and polytunnels – long, hooped greenhouses made of plastic sheeting – have all been positioned around what was the centre spot. This saves time and effort when getting water, young plants and organic matter to the vegetable-growing area.

Around this central area, the pitch has been dug over by the group and turned into strip beds. For ease of weeding and planting, these are no more than 1.4 m wide and have enough space between them to push a wheelbarrow.

The outer growing area is divided into five sections, large enough for growing a selection of cereals and green manure, as well as to provide enough grazing and hay for one cow and one ewe. In winter these are stalled in the team changing rooms, areas well used to witnessing animal behaviour.

Like all high-end football pitches, the ground is very sandy and fast-draining. So the survivors here are concentrating on growing crops that do well in light soils: things like potatoes, parsnips, carrots, onions, garlic and turnips. They've also planted some raspberries, as these are happiest in light, well-drained soil. And to protect the berries from birds? They've covered them with the goal nets.

NEED NO. 8
YOU

We've proved you *can* garden without a garden to garden in. You know what, though? You can't garden without a gardener. And that's where you come in.

Developing horticultural knowledge through the apocalypse will be the difference between your plants staying alive and you getting dead. It's that knowledge we'll discuss in the next chapter. But for now, congratulations. You have your seeds, your tools and your site.

You are ready to become a zombie gardener. ✷

DON'T GO THERE

GOOD ZOMBIE MOVIES, BAD GARDENING DECISIONS

Think you've landed the perfect zombie-gardening spot? Maybe. But some well-known apocalypse-survival sites are better than others

→

Spaceship greenhouses

In 1972, Douglas Trumbull's movie *Silent Running* showcased the almost perfect survival set-up: an attack-proof garden floating in space and tended by robots. Sealed in a glass geodesic bubble – imagine the Eden Project with fewer pensioners wandering about – it also pulled off the closed-loop coup de grâce, producing food without ever needing fertilizer brought in from elsewhere. Requires a spaceship to work, though, so unless you're Elon Musk it's a no-go.

ZOMBIE-GARDEN RATING 2/10

✦✦✩✩✩✩✩✩✩✩

Shopping malls

At first sight these certainly look tempting, filled as they are with store-cupboard staples and with only a few entry points to guard. Plus, like the mall in George A. Romero's *Dawn of the Dead* – and, yes, the actually pointless 2004 remake – they often have flat roofs large and sunny enough to grow veg in raised beds. Except – when did you last visit a shopping mall that sells compost, fertilizer and seeds? Exactly. Sadly, Tesco Extra and an H&M alone will not keep you alive. On the plus side, H&M stock some terrific cardigans.

ZOMBIE-GARDEN RATING 4/10

✦✦✦✦✩✩✩✩✩✩

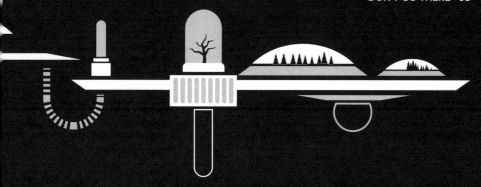

The whole of the Isle of Wight

In *The Day of the Triffids,* John Wyndham decided this fertile island was the best place to survive a mass-blinding-plus-killer-plants apocalypse. He wasn't wrong: the soil there is mostly slightly acid clay loam, there's a plant-friendly average annual rainfall of 870 mm[17] and lots of farming infrastructure to exploit.

But if even one zombie makes it onto the ferry from Portsmouth, you'll quickly find yourself trapped on the Isle of Fright. And France is a long swim away.

ZOMBIE-GARDEN RATING 7/10

✸✸✸✸✸✸✸✸✸✸

Gated communities

Big, comfortable houses with lots of lawn space for potential zombie gardens, all surrounded by ready-made security fencing? This could be the perfect spot to see out the apocalypse. Especially if like Alexandria, *The Walking Dead*'s suburban-survival spot, it has a handy central lake to use for irrigation/luring zombies to their doom. The big drawback? These are clearly brand-new houses, and twenty-first-century property developers nearly always make their gardens from a thin 10 cm of topsoil laid over a load of builder's rubble. You'll be dead before you've dug all that junk out.

ZOMBIE-GARDEN RATING 6/10

Secret underground laboratories and/or nuclear bunkers

Never mind that these are exactly the sort of spots where zombie outbreaks start, there's another problem. As stated on the tin: they're underground. If Milla Jovovich had wanted to eat fresh veg in *Resident Evil*, she'd have needed a set of full-spectrum lightbulbs to get her plants to grow. And where, in an apocalypse, is the electricity going to come from? Forget productive gardening, these kinds of sites are best left to now-insane AI and specially trained mutant commandos. Note: we don't know how or why computers go insane during apocalypses, but they do. We'd suggest that, instead of battling their way deep underground in an attempt to find and blow up the mad computer's master drive, the mutant commandos try switching it off and then switching it on again.

ZOMBIE-GARDEN RATING 1/10

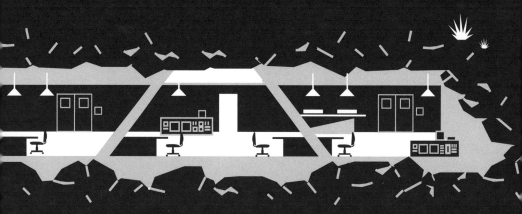

JUICE BAR IN A JIFFY

As you've seen by now, one of the keys to successful zombie gardening is to make maximum use of any outdoor space. How does that work before the apocalypse begins?

Let's say the only outside space you have is an empty balcony. As long as it's at least two metres wide and one metre deep, you've got room for five decent-sized containers. Maybe you're thinking 'But you told us veg plants are hungry – how will they grow in pots?' The answer is: they'll grow great. As long as you choose the right cultivars.

'Cultivar' is gardening shorthand for 'cultivated variety', meaning a plant that's been bred over generations to have particularly sweet fruit, give high yields – or, hooray, to grow particularly well in containers.

This means that if you choose the right cultivars, even on a balcony you can grow apples, blueberries, beetroot, kale and carrots: all the ingredients you need for a five-a-day-busting, vitamin C-packed smoothie.

Here's how.

1 START WITH AN APPLE

Sometime around early spring – mid to late February is ideal – you'll need to lay your hands on a young apple tree. There are about a billionty-million apple cultivars to choose from, but the one you want needs to be all of the following:

- The right size and shape for growing in containers
- Self-fertile, so it doesn't need another apple tree to pollinate it
- A 'midseason' variety, which means it'll be ready to harvest around the same time as the blueberries
- A variety that's good for juicing

Ask a nursery or garden centre for advice – but if they're too grumpy to help, just shout 'I want a three-year-old cordon-trained "Red Falstaff" on M26 or M9 rootstock and I want it now!' Which translates as: I would like a tree pruned into a space-saving, flat and upright shape, of a cultivar that produces good crops of juicy apples in late summer, growing on roots that restrict growth to the right size for a container. And I would like it now.

Plant your tree in a deep, 50 cm diameter pot in a weighty, soil-based compost, and then put it at the rear and middle of your chosen spot, where it won't shade the rest of your crops. Water regularly, and give it a drink of an all-purpose liquid fertilizer fortnightly until the end of August. By September the fruit will be ready to harvest: the apples will separate easily from the branch when you give them a gentle twist.

2 FIND A FRIENDLY BLUEBERRY

While you're buying the apple tree, pick up a blueberry bush too. The cultivar you're looking for should be:

- Self-fertile, to save space
- A late-season variety, so it crops at the same time as the apple

'Chandler' is worth a try, not least because then you could name the other four plants Monica, Rachel, Joey and Ross. Like all varieties of blueberry, it's basically a heavy-drinking acid-head, needing a constantly moist soil with a pH between 4.4 and 5.5 to survive.[18] So unless you live in the middle of a peat bog, you'll need to plant it in low-pH bagged compost: look for the kind that's labelled 'ericaceous'.

Use this to fill a pot that's at least 30 cm in diameter – it'll need to be this big to give the roots enough room – and stand it where it's least shaded by the apple: if your spot is south-facing, for instance, the pot should go directly in front of the tree. Feed every month from April to September with an ericaceous fertilizer, water with neutral-pH rainwater if possible and from midsummer on, you can begin to harvest: pick a little at a time, taking those berries that have turned from greenish-yellow to dark blue.

for this situation is a dwarf, curly-leaved cultivar like 'Afro'.

Kale only lives for a year, so it won't need as big a pot as the shrub or the tree: 20 cm deep and wide, filled with standard all-purpose compost or a soil and compost mix, will be fine.

Feed once a month from June to September with an all-purpose liquid fertilizer, keep it well watered and you should be able to harvest young leaves from late summer right through winter.

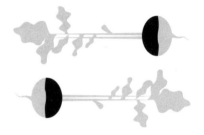

3 PLANT UP SOME KALE

Now turn your attention to the kale. You can either buy seed to sow in April, when the soil begins to warm up, or get young plants from garden centres in May, when they can go straight into pots. And yes we know this sounds a bit general – for detailed advice about sowing and growing your kale (as well as the beetroots and carrots), turn to Chapter 5.

Variety is still the key, as the standard-size kinds like 'Cavolo Nero' can be a bit top-heavy for a pot. Better

4 GET READY FOR BEETROOT

The next veg on your agenda is beetroot. Again, you can either buy young plants, or sow your seed in late May.

Some beetroot varieties are large-rooted for winter storing, others are cropped early at no more than golf-ball size. You want one that'll be ready with your other crops in September. That means going for a variety like Boltardy, which is less likely to grow crop-reducing flowers (a process known as bolting) through the hot, dry days of summer.

Another 20 cm by 20 cm pot, filled with an all-purpose potting compost, will be big enough to grow about six full-size plants. But do start with more: you can eat the extra roots as soon as they're 2 cm in diameter. Feed fortnightly with an all-purpose liquid fertilizer once the plants are 5 cm high, and keep moist: in hot weather and once the roots start to swell, you may need to water every day to stop them going woody.

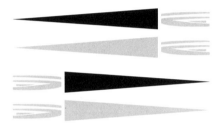

5 FINISH WITH CARROTS

The final pot is for carrots, which you'll need to sow in early June. (You might find young plants in garden centres, but we wouldn't bother: carrots don't respond well to being moved.) There are almost as many cultivars of carrots as of apples, but the one you want should be:

- Mid-length (i.e. with roots around six centimetres) so it doesn't feel cramped in a pot
- Main-season, so it'll still be cropping when the apples are ready
- Good for juicing

In our book, that means 'Bertan' or 'Mokum', but you don't have to take that as gospel.

Use a good deep container to give the roots room to develop – upwards of 30 cm would be ideal – and compost mixed with a little sand or grit to keep things light and draining freely. Sow the seeds directly into the pot, then, as carrots don't need quite as much sun as kale or beetroot, stand it in the shade of the blueberry bush.

The carrots shouldn't need feeding and aren't particularly thirsty – but don't let them dry out entirely or the roots will go woody. You can begin harvesting as soon as the roots are 1.5 cm thick, although they'll continue growing throughout the warm days of summer.

And that's pretty much it. Come September, you'll not only know exactly what 'cultivar' means, you'll be ready to fill your juicer/blender with super-fresh, home-grown fruit and veg and get a-pulping. And if afterwards you get fed up scrubbing pulp out of your juicer/blender, that's all the more reason to look forward to the apocalypse – when no one will expect you to make multi-ingredient health drinks and you can just damn well eat apples instead. ✳

3

GARDENING
IS WAR

Back in the sixties, the original grow-your-own brigade liked to make out that gardening was as simple as popping a bean in the ground one day and climbing a giant beanstalk the next. Read self-sufficiency manuals from that period and you'd think Mother Nature is on our side. Well, nature may be a mother. But she's the tricky, unstable kind. The type that bakes brownies, then hits the vodka and tries to get off with your best friend.

No, a better analogy is that nature is like Napoleon, endlessly adaptable and invasive. Nature doesn't want you to grow lovely things to eat. It wants to fill the world with its own mad and mostly inedible mixture of plants: first grass, then bushes and finally trees. Nature isn't flowers and harmony. Instead, like an episode of *I'm a Celebrity*, it's full of creepy crawlies, disease and ruthless competition.

Zombie gardeners get this. They know that in the battle to survive, it's vital you're familiar with both your friends and your enemies. So this chapter is here to help. In it, we'll take you through which plants are going to be most nutritionally useful, and why. We'll also show you how to identify and protect yourself against the most determined enemies of the zombie gardener, as well as how to spot the diseases that can finish a crop and, with it, your chances of survival.

But let's start with the good stuff: your chief apocalyptic allies. Aka plants.

Nature is like Napoleon, endlessly adaptable and invasive

FRIENDSHIP GROUPS

To adequately support yourself, you'll need to grow crops that meet different kinds of nutritional needs. And you'll need to do it in a way that provides food in every season. Luckily, veg plants divide up fairly neatly into three groups, each of which is good at doing a particular kind of food job at a particular time of year. Think of these groups as three friendly tribes, each of which you want fighting on your side.

The Carbohydrators: root vegetables

One of the most important plant tribes in the zombie garden are the root vegetables, which usefully store energy underground in swollen, carbohydrate-rich tubers or, yes, roots. Because they're often plants that grow rapidly in their first year then lie quietly in the cold winter soil before bursting back into life the following spring, root veg tend to store through winter well – as long as you keep them somewhere cool, dark and away from mice, rats and raiding parties from rival settlements.

This makes root veg an excellent source of carbohydrate-based calories in the autumn and winter, though some can be ready for harvesting and eating from early summer. Not all are equal, though. Some grow more roots or tubers per plant, others hold considerably more calories in each kilogram of crop. What really counts for zombie gardeners is how many calories you get from each kind of veg in a square metre of planting, as it'll help you decide how much space you should give them. You'll find out exactly how many plants of each kind of veg you can grow in a square metre when we get to Chapter 5. But in the meantime, take a look at

Tubers **look like roots, taste like roots, but are actually swollen sections of underground stem. A potato is a tuber; a beetroot is – surprise! – a root. It's only really worth knowing this if you want to show off to other zombie gardeners, or actively enjoy pub quizzes.**

HANDY TABLE NO. 2 ROOT VALUES

VEGETABLE	YIELD PER M²	KCAL PER M² [19]
Potatoes	10 kg[a]	7,700 kcal
Parsnips	4.85 kg[c]	3,637 kcal
Beetroots	5.8 kg[b]	2,494 kcal
Carrots	5.8 kg[b]	2,360 kcal
Turnips	6.3 kg[c]	1,764 kcal

the handy table above, which is based on how many calories there are in 100 g of each raw veg and average UK yields.

You'll see from this why spuds were traditionally the backbone of an allotment garden. Be warned, though: they don't crop well in every kind of soil and are prone to blight, an airborne fungal infection that blackens the leaves and turns the tubers to stinking slime. This is the same disease that caused the Irish potato famine in the nineteenth century, which led, after morally repugnant handwashing by the British, to the mass emigration of starving subsistence farmers to America, a whole load of recruits joining the ranks of the newly formed New York Police Department, and thus, in time, the chorus of 'Fairy Tale of New York'. The only bearable Christmas song ever written is thanks to potato blight, which shows that even apocalypses can have an upside.

Yield means the amount of food you crop from any planted area. Example usage: 'I'd keep the undead off your tomatoes if I were you – they're going to seriously reduce your yield.'

The Proteinators: peas and beans

Unlike root veg, peas and beans are all part of the same biological family: the legumes. As well as carrying seeds in pods, many legumes transform atmospheric nitrogen into plant food at special nodes on their roots – if you're not totally amazed by this, bear in mind that the human equivalent would be someone taking a lungful of oxygen, then having a slice of toast pop out of their trousers. What's more, some provide a third or more of their calories from proteins, and as protein is at a

A biological family is a group of plants that share a genetic heritage, and also a Latin name that can be really hard to remember. E.g. beetroot, chard and quinoa all belong to the Amaranthaceae family. Try saying that when you're being chased by a zombie.

premium in an apocalypse – Rick Grimes didn't get ripped without it – these plants are an important part of a zombie garden.

Peas and beans do two kinds of job. Some, like mangetout, sugar snap and garden peas, you eat when they're young, green and fresh. At this point their calorie and protein content are relatively low, so their main benefit is the fibre, vitamins and minerals they provide.

Others – like French, borlotti, broad, cannellini and runner beans – you can either eat young and green or harvest when

HANDY TABLE NO. 3 BEAN COUNTS

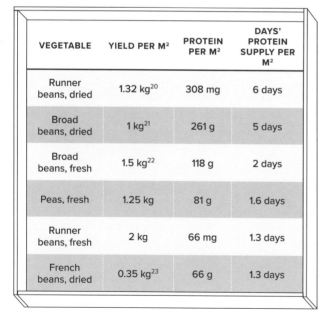

VEGETABLE	YIELD PER M²	PROTEIN PER M²	DAYS' PROTEIN SUPPLY PER M²
Runner beans, dried	1.32 kg[20]	308 mg	6 days
Broad beans, dried	1 kg[21]	261 g	5 days
Broad beans, fresh	1.5 kg[22]	118 g	2 days
Peas, fresh	1.25 kg	81 g	1.6 days
Runner beans, fresh	2 kg	66 mg	1.3 days
French beans, dried	0.35 kg[23]	66 g	1.3 days

the pods are dry and the beans/seeds inside fully mature. At this point they are at their most protein heavy and calorific, as the handy table on the left shows.

Reading this, you might think a zombie gardener should only bother growing beans for drying. But that would be to make two mistakes. First, fresh legumes are a good summer source of B vitamins and folic acid. The second is that you'd be relying on only one variety of veg. We can pretty much guarantee that, every year, one or more of your plantings will fail, wiped out by disease, unfriendly weather, pest attack or your own mistakes. The fewer types of crop you grow, the greater your potential percentage loss when something goes wrong. Just as zombie gardeners always carry several kinds of weapons when they move outside their secure perimeters, they always plant several kinds of veg.

The C-Section: brassicas

It won't matter how many varieties of veg you grow if a lack of vitamin C has made your teeth fall out. Which is why a well-stocked zombie garden needs to include plants that will provide your group with that vital vitamin – especially during winter. Traditionally, this was done

It won't matter how many varieties of veg you grow if a lack of vitamin C has made your teeth fall out

with the help of brassicas. Although, biologically speaking, swedes and turnips belong in this group, gardeners tend to think of brassicas as the leafy-greens crops: plants like kale, cabbage and broccoli. All provide good boosts of vitamin C, plus dietary fibre – important in an apocalypse, when toilet facilities tend to be the kind you don't want to hang around in.

Some of the brassicas are quite slow to crop, meaning that one sowing will occupy its patch of ground for a large part of the zombie-garden year. But you can always plant other, quicker-growing plants (known as catch crops) between their rows to maximize your food-to-space ratio. And, vitally, you often can harvest brassicas either in winter or in early spring, helping fill the hungry gap we talked about earlier.

You can also top up your vitamin C intake using fruit. From the first gooseberries in May to the last of the apples in October, berries, currants and top fruit crop across the warmer half of the year. But most come from shrubs and trees, which often take several years to start cropping properly – and time is short in a survival situation. So we'd suggest concentrating on just two:

- **Everbearing strawberries** The most C-heavy of traditional soft fruit grown outdoors in the UK, which crop from May through to early autumn from the first year you plant them.
- **Tomatoes** They may not have the most impressive C stats, but tomatoes are easy to preserve for winter eating by drying, canning or bottling. And yes, they are fruit: if you don't believe us, ask a biologist. Or just read the handy table below instead.

HANDY TABLE NO. 4 C THINGS CLEARLY

VEGETABLE	YIELD PER M²	VITAMIN C PER M²	DAYS' SUPPLY PER M²
Kale	2 kg	2,400 mg	60 days
Turnip greens	3.32 kg	1,995 mg	49 days
Cabbage	2.6 kg[24]	1,216 mg[25]	30 days
Tomatoes	7.8 kg	1,086 mg	26 days
Sprouting broccoli	1.2 kg	819 mg	20.5 days
Strawberries	1.35 kg	794 mg	20 days

You can see from all this that roots, brassicas and legumes will form the nutritional core of your zombie garden. But, like a single episode of *Stranger Things*, that is very far from the whole story.

The Outlanders: alliums, cucurbits and friends

Yes, three tribes. But vegetables within a tribe can belong to different families: carrots and potatoes might both be root veg, but carrots belong to the umbellifer family while potatoes belong to the solanums. And then there are other biologically related vegetable families you haven't even met yet. These include the alliums, such as garlic and onions; the cucurbits, such as squash and pumpkin; and the amaranths, such as leaf beet (aka perpetual spinach), chard and, yes, amaranth.

Why are these worth knowing about? Because between them they can add a whole lot of extra nutrients, like iron and vitamins A and B6, to your garden set-up. As we shall demonstrate with, inevitably, another handy table (right).

HANDY TABLE NO. 5 RELATIVE VALUES

VEGETABLE	FAMILY	YIELD PER M²	NUTRIENT	DAYS' SUPPLY PER M²
Chard	Amaranths	4.77 kg	Vitamin C	35 days
Squash	Cucurbits	3.6 kg[26]	Vitamin C	19 days
Courgettes	Cucurbits	1.92 kg	Vitamin B6	2 days
Garlic	Alliums	2.4 kg	Vitamin B6	20 days
Amaranth	Amaranths	4.34 kg[27]	Iron	9 days
Leaf beet	Amaranths	2 kg[28]	Iron	4.4 days
Carrots	Umbellifers	5.8 kg	Vitamin A	74 days
Lamb's lettuce	Valerians	540 g[29]	Vitamin A	8 days

Your Zombie Garden Backbone

In an ideal world, you'd maximize your nutritional spread by growing at least one vegetable from each tribe and each family. But not every zombie garden will have enough space. If you only have a few square metres to grow in, concentrate on what we call the seven backbone veg: those that give you the most calories for the space and the widest spread of vitamins, grow well even in containers and can be preserved easily or stored without refrigeration.

- Beetroot
- Carrots
- Dwarf beans
- Kale
- Onions
- Potatoes
- Tomatoes

Even if you find yourself starting the apocalypse with just a few pots on a patio, you can grow all of these seven plants as supplements to whatever you've managed to loot. That way you'll have most nutrients covered, as well as giving your diet a vital boost.

KNOW YOUR ENEMIES

Believe it or not, a zombie gardener has worse things to fear than actual zombies. Obviously a horde of the undead would be extremely destructive if they got into your crops, trampling plants and knocking them down. But there's a whole world full of feathered, clawed, hooved, slimy, sticky and properly alive enemies that will try to gain access to your garden and eat the hell out of it.

They're everywhere

Town or country, the following pests are likely to be a problem pretty much wherever you set up your zombie garden:

- **Birds** Blackbirds will pull up young onion plants by the tips, and strip fruit from trees and bushes the second it ripens. Pigeons will decimate brassicas. Crows will eat all your seed before it can germinate.
- **Mice and voles** Yes, they're cute. But also they're incredibly annoying. Mice (long tails, big ears) and voles (short tails, small ears) will tunnel through veg beds eating larger seeds, particularly peas and beans. They also pull off daring overnight raids in greenhouses and polytunnels, where they climb up bench legs, dig seeds out of pots and bite the heads off

germinated seedlings as if they were so many rows of lollipops. They're ridiculously acrobatic, too: about the only way to guarantee mice can't get to things is to hang them from somewhere high.

- **Cats** We've already established that cats think raised beds make great toilets. Spend hours raking a patch of soil to sow some seeds in, and you've just given them the keys to the executive bathroom.

Green and unpleasant

If you're surviving the apocalypse in the countryside, there's a whole extra set of pests to worry about – and as the human population falls, they'll expand their range into the cities, too.

- Wild boar Like small, hairy pigs crossed with a tractor. Incredibly destructive if they get in a zombie garden: they root up young fruit trees and bushes, and dig up and feast on potatoes.
- **Badgers** They're kind of endearing to look at – until they start rooting around for earthworms, flattening crops almost more effectively than a stray zombie. Unlike zombies, though, they're also partial to munching on beans, peas, potatoes, beetroot, strawberries and anything else with a hint of sweetness. And they're able to tear badger-shaped holes through pretty much all kinds of fencing.
- **Deer** Whether red, fallow, roe or muntjac, they will graze everything to bones. And we mean everything, from low-lying lettuce to apples high up in a tree. If they haven't eaten the tree already. Plus there's now estimated to be more deer living wild in the UK than in Tudor times.[30]
- **Rabbits** Bunnies are fluffy, cute and lethal. They will eat anything the deer forget, as long as they can reach it – and they can reach surprisingly high.

They will decimate anything green growing in the ground, but they also like to gnaw the bark off fruit bushes and the trunks of trees. That's the equivalent of flaying someone alive. No one mentioned that in *Watership Down*.

Spineless bastards

Next up is the invertebrate evil that is insects and molluscs – though we should point out that the majority of insects are a positive influence in the zombie garden. Many plants can't make fruit without first being pollinated by an insect, and for every bug pest, there will be another bug that either eats it or lays its eggs in it so its babies can eat it. (You thought the reproductive method in *Alien* was original? Insects have been bursting out of each other's stomachs for aeons.)

Boar are back: they're now well established in forests on the Welsh–English border, as well as in Kent and Sussex, and they may be getting a trotterhold in Devon and Dorset.

Even slugs and snails do some good by helping break down organic matter. But there are several that can cause serious damage to your crops. Here are some of the worst offenders:

- **Caterpillars** Some caterpillars are cool. Others are about as welcome in a veg garden as a murderous shape-changing entity in an Arctic research facility. The green-and-black offspring of the cabbage white butterfly, for instance, is basically the template for that children's book about the caterpillar that wouldn't stop eating: endlessly hungry, it will munch the leaves of kale, cabbage and broccoli to lace, seriously reducing their yield.

- **Blackfly** Not actually flies, but aphids: black shiny bug blobs that gather together and look a bit like caviar. They tend to appear on the juicy tips of fast-growing shoots and suck out their sap, making the new growth curl and wither. Delightfully, they can poo out female babies that are pregnant even before they're born.

- **Greenfly** Exactly like blackfly, except, well – green. Also with the pregnant-baby pooing.

- **Whitefly** Actual flies (i.e. they have wings) but really small: a whitefly infestation makes a plant look like it's got dandruff. The fly babies sit like small white limpets on the undersides of leaves and suck out all the sap. As if that weren't enough, black mould likes to grow on their excrement.

- **Carrot fly, cabbage root fly** Also actual flies. Love to lay their eggs around the bases of carrots and brassicas so that their maggot babies can eat the roots when they hatch.

- **Slugs** We've left the worst for last. Slugs are not just an enemy: they are *the* enemy. Slugs raze seedlings of every kind to the ground; rasp away mature leaves and stems of rhubarb, potatoes, beans, broccoli, peas, corn; tunnel through asparagus tips above ground, potatoes beneath. They're less keen on oniony and mustardy-flavoured things, but if that's all that's about, they'll wipe them out too. The only things we've never seen a slug eat are brambles and nettles. Which isn't much comfort – you can't survive on blackberries and nettle tea. Even in an apocalypse.

Thou shalt not pass

Traditionally, farmers' and market gardeners' answer to all of these pests was a bit like the end of any decent zombie movie: wholesale slaughter of everything that moved. Big pests would be shot; smaller ones were trapped or poisoned. On occasion they would be trapped *and* poisoned.

The trouble with bullets, pesticides and poisons is that, if you choose to use them, you'll have to make frequent trips off-site to restock – rarely a good idea in an apocalypse – and lootable supplies won't last for ever. Pesticides also have a habit of killing helpful creatures as well as harmful ones, and a time-poor zombie gardener will want nature to do as much of the work for them as possible, including getting one bug to eat another kind of bug.

Rather than going nuclear with broad-spectrum synthetic insecticides such as acetamiprid or deltamethrin (both of which are common ingredients in over-the-counter bug killers), squash greenfly, blackfly and whitefly with your fingers, or wash them away by spraying them with a solution of soft soap and vegetable oil in water. For just about everything else, we'd recommend you use what we'll call the barrier method. This doesn't mean plastering your garden in condoms but preventing pests from getting to crops using materials that are effective and almost endlessly reusable. Unlike condoms.

Different kinds of barriers do different jobs:

- **Black, woven-cord netting** This stops birds pecking at crops: you can sling it over poles topped with flower pots to protect brassicas, sweetcorn, fruit bushes and smaller fruit trees from attack.
- **Insect mesh** A white nylon fabric woven tightly enough to stop flies, butterflies, etc. from crawling through and laying their eggs on crops. Stretching it over rows of young brassicas in summer is pretty much vital if you aren't using insecticides.
- **Horticultural fleece** Not a jumper for middle-aged gardeners but a light, warm, semitransparent fabric you can lay over newly sown ground to stop birds eating seed. It's also handy for keeping frost off vulnerable plants in early spring and winter.

Before the apocalypse, all of these products were sold by the metre, and the bigger garden centres and country stores usually had a section displaying them on large, cut-your-own-length rolls. Take bolt cutters with you when you loot and you can remove entire rolls from their display racks: simple.

ZOMBIES ARE TRUE, THIS ISN'T

NO. 1 'YOU DON'T NEED CHEMICALS TO STOP SLUGS'

Now, we know what we just said about poisons, barrier protection, etc., etc. But the only thing that gets rid of slugs is slug pellets. And before an army of organic gardeners starts tearing our heads off, we're not saying pellets are the only things that kill slugs. Quite a lot of things kill them. E.g.:

- If you bury a glass of beer in the soil at the end of a potato patch, it will, yes, be full of alcohol-poisoned slugs by morning.
- If you sprinkle them with salt, they will, yes, curl up and die.
- If you go out at night wearing a head torch and armed with a pair of scissors or a knitting needle, you can, yes, pick slugs off individual plants and either stab them or snip them in half. (NB: This is a good job for children or other survivors too weak to help with killing zombies.)

That's all fine. Except that a well-cultivated soil, rich in moisture-retentive OM, can easily host a population of 250 slugs in every square metre.[31] In even the smallest zombie garden, that's more beer, salt or child-with-scissors hours than you'll likely have to spare.

If you spent any time before the apocalypse reading gardening blogs – which, being functionally alive, you probably didn't – you'll know how much gardeners like to discuss non-chemical methods of stopping slugs crawling towards plants. Copper tape, gravel, soot, Vaseline, egg shells, coffee grounds, sheep's wool, yadda yadda yadda. None of them works – or not well enough. Slugs don't appear to actively enjoy crossing a thick circle of coffee grounds to get to a lettuce, but in our experience, if they're hungry and the lettuce is juicy, they'll grit their sluggy teeth (actually, a sort of horrible scrapy tongue called a radula) and slime across

anyway. In essence, slugs are like a stalker you met on Tinder. One coffee or a beer isn't going to put them off. Even if you resort to drowning them and/or setting them on fire, the next day they're back again.

What should a smart zombie gardener do? Well, first of all, they can keep their seedlings on a table with its legs standing in beer-filled trays, so that slugs get too pissed to climb up for a nibble in the night. They won't use nitrogen-rich liquid fertilizers, which encourage plants to put on juicy, soft top growth – crack cocaine for slugs. They won't use straw to mulch their soil, because that's like making a five-star hotel for molluscs; nor will they grow young plants through holes in black plastic weed fabric, because that's like providing a top-end, slug-friendly Airbnb.

Instead, they will lift up pots every other day to inspect their bottoms for baby slugs, which they will squish. They will also go outside on rainy days and stomp grown-up slugs to mush as they slither across the grass. And they will do everything they can – including digging a pond – to encourage the ducks, frogs, slow-worms and toads that predate slugs.

But what they will also do – at sowing time, and when plants are very young and vulnerable – is use organic, ferric-sulphate slug pellets. Only as many and as often as it says on the packet, and only when if they don't, they're going to lose their crop. Otherwise they will starve, and zombies will walk the earth triumphant.

Mulch is a thick, protective layer of organic matter which you pile onto the soil after planting. It's also the word 'much' with an 'l' in it.

SICK BASTARDS

The final enemies you'll have to contend with are invisible: the bacteria, viruses and fungal spores that cause a whole encyclopaedia of plant diseases. Microscopic organisms like *Fusarium*, *Sphaerotheca* and *Phytophthora* are not only impossible to spell, they reduce yields and in some cases wipe out whole crops.

Some are like the zombie virus: once a plant has been infected, it's a goner and you might as well dig it out and burn it before it has a chance to infect its friends. Other diseases plants can survive, though in a weakened state. And sometimes what looks like disease is actually just a symptom of malnutrition – the plant doesn't have enough water or is missing something in its diet.

To show you what we mean, here's a game we like to play called 'Dead, Diseased, Deficient'. Look at the table on the right, identify the symptom your plant is displaying, and then decide whether there's something you can do to help — or whether it's time to book the funeral directors.

FUN GAME NO. 1 (ACTUALLY, THE ONLY FUN GAME)

DEAD, DISEASED, DEFICIENT

SYMPTOM	DEAD, DISEASED OR DEFICIENT?	ACTION
Potato leaves develop soft, black blotches which rapidly spread; eventually the plant collapses	Diseased and dead: it's been attacked by late blight fungus	None. The tubers will inevitably rot. Dig up the whole lot and burn them
Potato leaves go yellow in the middle, then small, crispy brown patches appear between their veins	Deficient: there's a lack of magnesium available in the soil	Spray the leaves with a solution of Epsom salts, or add more compost/ manure at planting time next year
Leaves of all the peas in a row go soft and floppy	Deficient: lack of water means they're wilting	Water them. Duh
Bottom leaves of some pea plants in a row turn yellow, tops begin to wilt and watering doesn't help	Diseased and dead: fusarium wilt fungus is rotting the roots	Pull out affected plants. Be careful not to damage the roots of those nearby
Surfaces of pea leaves go greyish-white and powdery	Diseased and deficient: lack of water at the roots gives the go-ahead to powdery mildew fungus to infect wet top growth	Pick off affected leaves, and water at the base, not from overhead. Yield may be a bit reduced, but the plant should survive

Learning to identify plant diseases is tricky. But well-grown, unstressed plants are much less susceptible to attack – pests and diseases, like packs of wolves, always seem to pick off the weakest first. As long as you have the skills to sow and grow vegetables well, you'll reduce your losses to all these beasts.

Which is where the next chapter comes in. But first, let's see how your team are coping as that first apocalyptic winter closes in. ✳

NO FUELLING YOU

POST-PETROL
POWER OPTIONS

Your team has made it out of town and found a site, but the electricity is out. For good. What are your options for powering up and keeping warm?

→

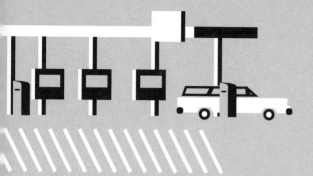

Looted fuel

In zombie movies, there always seems to be fuel to run car engines and electricity generators – even though there's no one around to work the oil rigs, run refineries, drive tankers or work the tills at petrol stations without making eye contact. The truth is, in airtight containers, petrol and diesel stay usable for only a year. In a car's tank, petrol's volatile compounds begin to evaporate, and it'll only last a measly four weeks. Diesel doesn't evaporate so quickly, but after a few months in a car's tank or an unsealed container, fungi and bacteria will have degraded it so much it will be barely any use. Even if you find an abandoned tanker or two to drive back to your compound, after a year or so you won't be able to use them to power up your camp – or run machinery in the garden.

SURVIVAL RATING 2/5

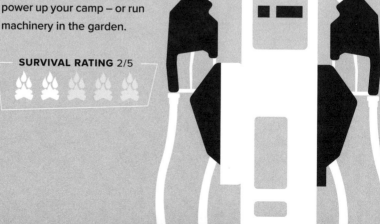

GYO PPO

Even before the apocalypse, engines could run on pure plant oil (PPO). Handily, a square metre of oilseed rape – anyone who's driven down a motorway in May will have seen fields full of its bright yellow flower – will make 160 ml of PPO.[32] But you need a tractor to plough, sow and harvest it. And a specialized machine to press the seed and extract the oil. And 112 litres of from-the-pump diesel per hectare of oilseed rape to run the tractor and the specialized machine.[33] And a fuel preheater and/or a heated fuel filter for each engine you want to run. And someone who knows what a fuel preheater and/or a heated fuel filter is.

In other words, growing your own PPO is an ace option. But only if you are a fully qualified garage mechanic who happens to be surviving on a farm.

SURVIVAL RATING 3/5

Chop up your chintz

Let's assume your survival site comes fitted with a wood-burning stove (you're in Fulham, right)? Hooray, you'll be keeping warm with wood! But before you rush out and start chopping down trees, consider this. Wood needs to be seasoned, or dried out, to burn properly. If you have a store of new wood, you need to leave it, ideally in a dry place, for up to two years. Also, you'll need quite a lot of it. Heat is measured in British thermal units (BTU): one BTU is roughly the amount of heat given off by a single match. The average UK house uses about 44 million BTU a year.[34] That's a lot of matches.

To save on Swan Vestas, take your lead from the we're-surviving-in-a-library scene in *The Day After Tomorrow* and start by burning all your wooden furniture. Because it's been inside, it will be properly seasoned, aka dry enough to burn efficiently. And as a kilogram of dry wood will hold about 13,700 BTU of useable heat,[35] if you weigh your furnishings, you can judge pretty exactly how much heat they will provide.

To keep an average room warm for one year, you should fill your stove with:

- Two hundred and eleven 3.82 kg JOKKMOKK pine dining chairs from Ikea, or
- Thirty-three 24 kg solid oak dining benches from Roseland, or
- Eight 97 kg solid teak sideboards from Tikamoon

Only once you've burnt your furniture, and the furniture in your dead neighbours' homes, and the furniture in Furniture Warehouse, should you turn to option number four: trees.

SURVIVAL RATING 4/5

Street legal

Plant one and a half acres with fast-growing willow, and yippee, you'll have enough wood to heat your house year after year.[36] But that's going to be one and a half acres more than town survivors will have. They will have to rely on chopping up street trees, the kind planted by now-extinct councils.

Logs from street trees will have different qualities depending on the species they came from. Some will burn slowly, some fast. Split, stacked and stored properly, some will be seasoned after just a few months. Others need the full two years. Ideally, you want to use a mixture of slow- and fast-burning species and slow- and fast-seasoning species. Also consider that small and medium-size trees will be easier and safer to fell.

In England, the five most common street trees are, in descending order, maple, cherry, rowan, birch and whitebeam.[37] And guess what? Maple, cherry, rowan, birch and whitebeam are all small or medium-sized trees and a mix of fast and slow burners. Plus, while cherry takes a long time to season, the others can be ready to use within a few months. It's as if the now-extinct councils knew what was coming.

SURVIVAL RATING 5/5

BREAD IN A BED

We have some bad news for you, people. In an apocalypse, Greggs will be closed. If you fancy a sandwich, you'll have to grow your own wheat.

Cereal crops are, essentially, just overbred grass: once you know that, a field of wheat just looks like a lawn that's been to the gym too often. But better, because you don't have to mow it and it turns into baguettes. Luckily, wheat isn't much harder to grow than grass – even in containers. This means you can practise your cereal-crop skills well before civilization collapses. Here's how.

1 SOURCE YOUR SEED

Winter wheat seed, which you sow in September/October and harvest roughly nine months later, is the kind to look for. Some veg-seed companies (see Resources, page 214) stock the kind of wheat seed that's good for bread-making flour, or you could ask an agricultural seed supplier to sell you what are known as trial packs, in 1 kg or 5 kg bags. But don't bother with the wheatgrass seed you'll see sold online. This is, yes, wheat, but won't necessarily be the kind that has a high-enough protein content to make a decent loaf.

2 CHOOSE YOUR SPOT

For 360 g flour, enough to make a sandwich loaf, you'll need half a square metre of growing space[38] in a nice sunny area: a corner of a well-dug, weed-free garden bed would be good, or a couple of deep containers — two 56 cm diameter pots will give you roughly half a square metre of growing space. Don't try to use growbags or a shallow bed on a roof or patio, though, as wheat likes to get its roots deep — in some cases as far as two metres down.[39]

3 PREPARE THE GROUND

Wheat yields best in soils with a pH of 6.5, so if yours is very acid, raise the pH with lime a couple of weeks before sowing, then rake the soil over until it is very fine and crumbly. If you're growing in containers, fill them with an all-purpose compost.

Horticultural lime is not a less useful relative of lemons but a finely ground stone used by gardeners to make soil more alkaline. Wood ash will do nearly as good a job.

4 SOW AND PROTECT

If the soil is dry, water the bed or container, then scatter 8 g of wheat seeds (roughly 166 seeds, if you're counting) across the soil surface:[40] sown this close, they should shade out any weeds that try to get established. Cover with 5 cm of soil[41] either by raking or shaking compost through a sieve, then water gently. It's autumn, so you probably won't need to water much more – but don't let the soil dry out entirely.

Stop birds and squirrels eating the seed by keeping some fleece over the surface of the soil until you see the first shoots emerge. This should take between five and fourteen days, after which you have to go on full slug alert, at least until the young plants are 10 cm high.[42]

5 GIVE IT A FEED

Growth will be slow until late February, when the wheat plants will suddenly start to shoot up. This is the moment to scatter a leaf-boosting fertilizer like pelleted chicken manure among your young plants. Do this again in late March, then give a dose of liquid tomato fertilizer in May – this will contain the right nutrients to help the ears, or seed heads, form. After that, don't feed, or the wheat might grow too high and 'lodge' – aka fall over on itself.

6 HARVEST AND DRY

The wheat will be ready to harvest sometime between June and August, once the stalks are turning brown and the grains of wheat don't dent when you press a fingernail into them. Discard any with ears that look shrivelled, blackened or mouldy, as they could be infected with the fungi that cause ergot or fusarium head blight, neither of which are things you want in your dinner. Cut the stalks close to the soil surface and hang them upside down somewhere airy to dry.

7 BASH AND GRIND

Now you need to thresh, or separate, the grain from its hulls. We won't lie, this is hard work, and you may need to repeat 'steak bake, jam doughnut and tuna mayo sub' to keep yourself motivated. Put your dried wheat stalks into a pillowcase and bash them with a stick or a length of hose. Or lie them on some kind of ridged surface – a rubber doormat, say – and trample on them.

To get rid of all the bits of unwanted hull and other debris, lay a bedsheet or tarp on the floor in front of an electric fan. (There are manual ways of doing this, as you'll discover in the next chapter, but while you've got the tools you might as well use them.) Stand a bucket or similar in front of the fan, switch it on and then slowly pour the contents of the pillowcase into the container: the fan will blow away all the light, unwanted stuff, while the grain will land in the bucket.

Now you can grind it into flour: a manual coffee mill will do the job, or a good-quality kitchen blender. Kept somewhere cool, dark and dry, the leftover grain should stay viable and sandwich-worthy for several years. So long, Greggs, it was nice eating you. ✳

SOLDIER SKILLS

Now that you know what to grow, you need to know *how* to grow it. Which is, to be fair, quite a big subject.

Sowing your seeds, improving your soil, fertilizing your plants – there's a lot to learn and, in an apocalypse, not a lot of time to learn it in. Unlike Keanu Reeves who, in *The Matrix*, got to download his know-how by sticking a hosepipe into the back of his neck, you're going to have to gather information the hard way, by reading this book. So to keep things simple – and, yes, to make it feel a bit like you're training to be a sacred warrior with total control over body, mind and other people's bullets – we've divided the following chapter into eight key skills. All of which the successful zombie gardener needs to master. Don't despair, though – they're are lot easier to learn than Keanu's full skill-set:

> There's a lot to learn and, in an apocalypse, not a lot of time to learn it in

- Kung fu, ju-jitsu and judo
- The ability to punch through boards from a distance of 5 cm
- Stripping and rebuilding a machine gun blindfolded
- Killing people with a pencil
- Bending reality with the power of his mind while wearing a long leather coat
- Maintaining a full head of hair well into middle age
- Acting while sitting down, and standing up

So take the red pill, not the blue pill, and let's get going.

SKILL NO. 1

IMPROVING YOUR SOIL

The food you grow can only ever be as good as the soil it's grown in. Any time you spend nurturing soil – feeding it, encouraging microorganisms to live in it, protecting it from exposure to wind and rain – is like money in the bank for your plants. Money that they pay back with interest at harvest time.

Keeping that slightly annoying analogy going, a top-earning hedge-fund soil would have an open, airy, but still moisture-retaining structure that roots can move through easily, and be teeming with earthworms, fungi and bacteria that turn decaying vegetable matter into plant food. It would also be neither too acid nor too alkaline, have a good balance of all the different nutrients a plant needs and be based in an office in St James's with allocated parking for two Porsches and a Merc. OK, not the last bit. But you can see what we're getting at.

All but the luckiest zombie gardeners will have to work to achieve that ideal growing medium, opening up a heavy clay soil so it's not so tightly packed or thickening a sandy soil so nutrients don't wash through it like a sieve. In both cases the easiest, most effective way to do this is to add organic matter (OM).

This comes in three main forms, which you can use singly or mingle together:

- **Garden compost** A mix of well-rotted grass clippings, twigs, woodchips, paper and cardboard, fruit and veg peelings, straw and rubbish from the garden
- **Leaf mould** Well-rotted deciduous leaves (the kind that drop in autumn)
- **Farmyard manure** A mix of well-rotted cow and/or sheep poo

Well-rotted OM can be dug into the top 10–25 cm or so of soil in late winter or early spring at a rate of roughly a ten-litre bucketful to every square metre. If it's less well-rotted – for complicated reasons to do with nitrogen uptake that we won't bore you with – you spread it on warm soil in late spring and let the worms drag it in for you.

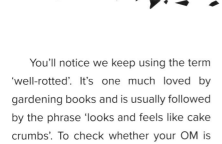

You'll notice we keep using the term 'well-rotted'. It's one much loved by gardening books and is usually followed by the phrase 'looks and feels like cake crumbs'. To check whether your OM is well-rotted or not, use this handy table:

HANDY TABLE NO. 6

HAVE YOUR CAKE AND SPREAD IT

LOOK AND FEEL	ROT STATUS
Looks and feels like cake crumbs	Well-rotted
Looks and feels like bits of twigs/old leaves	Not well-rotted
Looks, feels and tastes like cake crumbs	Cake crumbs

Compost corner

In even the smallest zombie garden, a bucket of OM per metre adds up to – well, a whole heap. Which is why you'll probably want to build a heap of your own: a compost heap.

Entire books have been written about making compost, but the basics are simple enough.

- Make your heap as big as you can – ideally no less than one cubic metre, so that the heat produced from decomposition stays put and speeds up rotting.
- Mix roughly one-third juicy green stuff (e.g. grass, nettle tops, veg-garden discards) with two-thirds dry brown stuff (e.g. cardboard, sawdust, twigs, straw).
- Keep the mix just barely moist – definitely not soaking wet, and not bone dry either.
- Turn it all over every now and again to let air in and help it rot evenly.

If you chop everything up small first and have the willpower and muscle-power to turn the heap every six weeks or so, you'll have useable compost in six months. If not, it'll take about a year to be bucket ready.

Go green

There is another method of improving soil, and one that we reckon is brilliant in or out of an apocalypse: using green manures. These are annuals you sow into bare soil immediately after harvesting and clearing away a crop. You leave the plants to grow, usually over winter, then cut them down before they flower, chop them up and dig the whole lot into the top 10–25 cm[43] of soil about a month and a half[44] before sowing or planting your next batch of veg.

Green manures such as blue lupin, sweet clover and field beans have penetrating roots that break up soil better than any garden fork, while thick-growing Italian ryegrass and fodder rye protect soils from washing away in the winter wind and rains. Used the right way, some of them can help raise fertility levels (see Feeding, page 112). But all of them add OM to the soil without – and this is the killer – you having to move around barrowloads of heavy compost or animal shite. Green manure is good for your garden, and even better for your back.

ZOMBIES ARE TRUE, THIS ISN'T

NO. 2 'YOU DON'T HAVE TO DIG'

As the apocalypse wears on and you spend the long dark evenings behind your nailed-up front door reading gardening books, you may well come across something called the 'no dig' method of improving ground. Traditionally gardeners spent a lot of time digging. Turning the ground over to roughly the depth of a fork or spade head before sowing or planting got it all nice, fluffy and root friendly, gave you the chance to incorporate lots of OM and also meant you'd remove any weeds. No-dig gardening, on the other hand, avoids disturbing soil wherever possible, maintaining not only its natural structure – which no-dig fans argue is spoilt when you turn it over with a spade or fork – but also keeping intact a network of tiny fungal threads, known as mycorrhiza, that weave through the soil and move nutrients from one place to another.[45]

Instead of forking soil over each spring, these veg growers leave the ground untouched and instead cover it with 5–7.5 cm of well-rotted OM, typically in early winter. The following spring they plant directly into this, leaving the plant roots to romp through the top layer of OM before growing down into and breaking up the less forgiving ground beneath. Done properly, even on unpromising soils like sand or very wet clay, the results can be excellent.

But. *But*. To build a layer 7.5 cm deep, you need around seventy-five litres of OM per square metre: enough to almost fill a heavy-duty wheelbarrow. Even the most math-deficient can see that any time and energy you might have saved on spadework will be spent filling and emptying barrows of compost instead. More importantly, a one-cubic-metre compost heap will rot down into about three hundred litres of finished material – enough for just four square metres of no-dig garden. For anyone with more than a very small site, sourcing enough on-site material is likely to be pretty problematic.

So we reckon unless you have easy access to a mountain of manure, save this method for small areas and for plants that don't need a very deep layer of airy, stone-free soil to crop well: beetroot or onions, say. For everything else: keep digging.

SKILL NO. 2

SOWING AND GROWING

As soon as the apocalypse begins, you're going to need to start sowing seed. That's because most of the crops in a zombie garden need to be grown each year from scratch.

Some, like parsnip seed, you sow outside in the patch of soil where they'll stay until cropping time: this is called sowing direct. But in most cases, you'll lose fewer crops to pests and bad weather if you sow seed in those module trays you looted, and nurture them until the weather outside is reliable enough not to kill young plants off.

Because not all seeds are born equal, they need different temperatures to germinate. This means you'll need to provide your modules with some kind of shelter. In an apocalypse, the form that shelter takes will vary, as the handy table on the right shows.

Whichever of the shelter options below you go for, what you are doing is known to gardeners as 'sowing under cover'. For example: germinating

HANDY TABLE NO. 7 GERMINATE! GERMINATE!*

GERMINATION SOIL TEMPERATURE	PRE-APOCALYPSE OPTION	POST-APOCALYPSE OPTION
Hot 21° C+	Heated, lidded electric propagator with thermostatic temperature control	Tea tray next to the oven
Warm 16–21° C	Greenhouse or polytunnel	Shelving unit stood against an outside wall and covered in bubble wrap
Cool 8–16° C	Purpose-built cold frame	Clear plastic storage box with the lid propped open

* Read this in a Dalek voice.

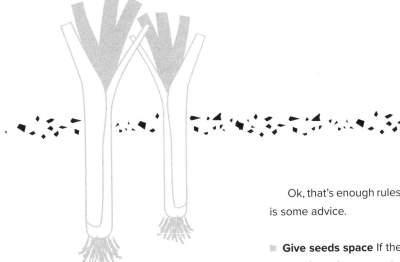

seeds in a heated propagator or on a windowsill means you are growing under cover. Germinating them in a heated propagator or on a windowsill in the MI6 building means you are growing under cover undercover. (Though this is a rubbish joke. Because everyone *knows* it's the MI6 building, right?)

Wherever you sow, some rules are always the same.

- **Rule No. 1** Sow at the right time and the right depth.
- **Rule No. 2** Most seeds do best sown sometime between twelve and sixteen weeks before the last frosts and no deeper than their own size.
- **Rule No. 3** Rule No. 2 is so rough it's actually useless. Much better is to look at Chapter 5, where we give precise sowing instructions for each zombie vegetable.

Ok, that's enough rules. Here instead is some advice.

- **Give seeds space** If they're too close together, they can stop each other from germinating or growing well. This is why seed packets often say 'sow thinly' – without ever actually saying how thin thinly is. This is almost as helpful as saying 'one of our customer service representatives will be with you as soon as possible'.
- **Get seeds in good contact with the growing medium** This way they stand the best chance of absorbing the moisture they need for germination while their baby roots (known as radicles) can get a good grip.
- **Water seeds, don't drown them** Germination needs moisture to begin. But if you water too vigorously, seeds will get washed away.
- **Don't let seeds dry out** It'll stop germination, and once it's stopped, it might not restart.

How all this plays out in practice will look something like the handy table overleaf.

HANDY TABLE NO. 8 SOW SO

	OUTSIDE	UNDER COVER
Step 1	Rake soil back and forth at right angles until you have a a fine, crumbly layer of soil about 2.5 cm deep (this is known as a 'tilth').	Use a bagged seed compost, or make a finely sieved mix of equal parts leaf mould, washed sharp sand and topsoil.
Step 2	Draw out rows in the tilth to the recommended sowing depth. If soil is really soggy, sprinkle a thin layer of sand across the bottom of the row.	Fill containers with compost, then knock the containers a couple of times on a hard surface to settle out big air pockets.
Step 3	Pre-water rows using a very fine rose.	Pre-water containers by standing them in gravel trays full of water then removing and letting them drain. Gently tamp down the compost surface with a piece of wood, or use the base of a pot the same size as the one you've sown in.
Step 4	Drop in seeds.	Place seeds on the surface.
Step 5	Use a rake to draw dry soil back across the row, and tamp down gently with the back of the rake head.	Sieve compost over the seeds to the recommended depth, then gently firm again using the tamper/pot.
Step 6	Cover with horticultural fleece to protect the seed bed.	Cover with sheets of glass or plastic bags to keep humidity high. Place somewhere with the right germination temperature.
Step 7	Wait two weeks, then, when nothing happens, start crying.	Water carefully every other day for a week. Then forget for forty-eight hours, during which time the seeds all germinate, dry out and die. Start crying.

The difficult teenage years

Germinating seeds is like having children: you think once you've done the giving-birth bit, you're home and dry. Not so much.

First off, you have to get the light levels right. The minute germinated seeds poke their heads above ground, they'll be relying on UV light to give them strength. Inside or out, take any coverings off as soon as you see green shoots, and make sure module trays are getting light from all directions. Be careful, though: too much direct sun when they're this young will make them shrivel and die like vampires. And too little light will mean they etiolate, or go all pale and floppy. Also like vampires.

You have to keep a very close eye on watering, too. Too much and roots suffocate; too little and the tops shrivel. If humidity is too high, seedlings can 'damp off': succumb to a fungal attack that turns the base of the stems to slime. Then of course there are the usual enemies. All a seedling consists of is a single root and two specialized leaves called cotyledons. These are nearly always fat and round, like lovely little baby cheeks. Don't you just want to nibble them? Yes, and so do slugs.

Following the old agricultural advice that the best medicine is the farmer's footprint, the most useful thing you can do with seedlings is check on them often, every day if you can. That way you have the best chance of stepping in and preventing a minor problem from becoming a crop-destroying catastrophe.

Also, keep 'em moving. Yes, seedlings look incredibly fragile, and you might be tempted to let them stay put. But seed compost deliberately has very few nutrients, and seedlings crowded together won't have enough light and space to grow properly. So once seedlings have developed their first pair of true, adult leaves (the next pair to grow after the baby cotyledons), they're ready for something called 'pricking out': not a slogan on a Women's March placard, but the process of moving seedlings into bigger pots so that they have room to develop good root systems.

Cotyledons are also known as 'seed' or 'untrue' leaves, and they always come in pairs. Apart from when they don't: leeks, onions and garlic throw up a single cotyledon that looks like a very thin blade of grass.

How to prick out

First, get your upgrades ready: choose individual pots a couple of centimetres wider and deeper than the modules, and fill them either with bagged potting compost, which has more nutrients than seed compost, or a homemade mix of equal parts sieved garden compost, topsoil and leaf mould.

Tap the pot to settle the contents a little without squashing out all the air, then prod a small hole in the compost surface. Dig a teaspoon or a two-pronged fork into the soil of the module and gently lever each seedling out of its birthplace. Then, holding the seedling by one of its cotyledons – not the stem or an adult leaf, they're too precious and easy to damage – lower it into the hole in its new pot.

Shake the pot gently to settle the compost round the roots, then give it a good water (but use a very fine rose, which will also help wash away any clogging bits of soil on the seedling's leaves). Keep pricked-out seedlings out of direct sunlight for the first twenty-four hours, to give them a chance to get over their moving-day trauma.

Next, watch for roots. After a few weeks, gently tap one of your seedlings out of its pot and check how well the root system is developing. If you can see only a few fine white threads down there, put it back and leave it to grow a little longer. But if the edges of the soil are showing a clear network of roots – about as thick as the London Underground map combined with local Overground links – it's time to either pot your plant on into a bigger container or get it ready to fly the nest. Which means it's time for skill no. 3.

SKILL NO. 3
PLANTING OUT
AND PROTECTING

Seedlings that have germinated and grown in open ground are used to wind, direct sun and battering rain. Like anyone who went to a school with an Ofsted rating of 'satisfactory', they're survivors.

But plants grown under cover have led sheltered lives. They are, literally, softies: their green tissues are juicy and fragile, and if they're chucked into the real world too abruptly, they will, like a certain kind of public school boy, collapse.

Before they can leave their pots and be planted outside, they need to be hardened off. How? Put them in a cold frame. Traditionally this was a low, brick-built structure sited against a south-facing garden wall or side of a greenhouse, with timber and glass lids a gardener could raise during the day to expose young plant tissue to wind, strong sunlight and lower temperatures. For the first week or so they'd close the lids at night to keep the plants from having to deal with too great a fluctuation in temperature, but for the second week they'd leave the lids raised at night too. After a fortnight or so of this treatment, the plants were ready.

Not many zombie-garden sites come with ready-made cold frames. But building a DIY version isn't difficult – you can make one out of wooden pallets and old window frames easily enough. Or just stand young plants outside somewhere sheltered from wind and direct sunlight, and for the first week, cover them with a double layer of fleece at night.

Hardening off means stressing the soft tissues of plants grown under cover to prep them for life in the outdoors. A bit like Tough Mudder, except with a point.

Always use protection

Once your plants have good root systems and are properly hardened off, it's time to plant them out. Using a trowel or a dibber – a long, strong stick with one pointy end – make a series of holes at the recommended planting distances for whatever veg you're putting out. Remove plants from their pots by laying the flat of your hand across the top of each pot, turning it upside down and giving it a smart tap on the bottom. Carefully drop the plants into their holes so that the tops of their root balls are level with the rest of the soil, and firm them in by gently pressing the soil down around them. This, and the thorough watering you knew we were going to tell you to now give them, helps make sure the young roots make good contact with the soil.

Planting distances affect yield, so check Chapter 5 to see how many plants to grow in a square metre. Then you can choose whether to grow them in blocks, which saves space, or rows, which makes weeding easier.

Plants are vulnerable throughout their lives to attacks from predators, but they're never more vulnerable than when you first plant them out. They're still small, and just a couple of bites from a snail, rabbit or whatever will pretty much finish them off. Also predators seem to be like the rest of us: whenever there's something new on the menu, they get excited and go on a binge. Whether the next day they feel full of self-loathing and spend two hours at a spin class we don't know; but what's for sure is that slugs, pigeons and mice can destroy a row of new plants in a single night. So the minute you've planted out, protect, protect, protect.

- Fence young plants with twigs of different sizes to discourage cats and birds.
- Lay spiky holly branches across the earth to make it uncomfortable for mice.
- Plant among a thick stand of leafy 'sacrifice' seedlings – Swiss chard, say – to distract slugs.

What about cloches – those off-the-shelf hard plastic tunnels or domes you peg down into the soil over young plants? Keen-eyed zombie gardeners will have spotted that we kept them off

Hoop for the best

To make a protective cloche tunnel, first collect some thick twigs, lengths of bamboo or, if you can get it, reinforced steel bar. Push these as deep as you can into the earth every 60 cm or so on either side of the plants you want to protect.

Then push the ends of a length of MDPE water pipe (the blue kind you find at builder's supply shops) over opposite pairs of the supports to make an upright semicircular hoop a little taller than your plants – about 60 cm high will be enough for most crops. Do this along the whole row.

Next, stick two bamboo canes into the soil by the middle of each hoop, one on either side. Slant them so their tops cross to make a V shape, and fix them together with garden string or a cable tie. If you sit the apex of the hoop into this V, the canes will help stop the cloche collapsing and squashing plants in bad weather.

Now drape all your hoops with a single piece of fleece, insect mesh or polytunnel plastic sheeting. Pull this as tight as you can to stop it sagging on top of the plants, then weigh the long sides down with bits of timber, stones, old roof tiles or bricks. Close the ends off by pulling the covering material together and weighing it down.

the looting lists. Why? Well, the domes are okay for protecting a few plants in small gardens – but it's just as easy to cut old plastic drinks bottles in half and use them instead. And the open-ended tunnels you put on rows of veg are only good for creating a bit of extra warmth. In every other way, they are just like putting a buffet table in a wedding marquee on a rainy day: everyone heads there for dinner. We reckon it's quicker, more economical and more effective to build your own closed-end tunnels using home-made cloche hoops.

SKILL NO. 4
FEEDING

Plants need regular feeding, just like animals in a zoo. Feeding a plant is a lot less entertaining than feeding a dolphin, though. PlantWorld is never going to compete with SeaWorld. But on the plus side, a plant isn't going to lose its marbles if you keep it in a confined place, and no one was ever prosecuted for mistreating a potato.

At the top of plants' food list are three chemical elements: nitrogen, which is vital for green top growth; phosphorus, which is particularly important in establishing good root systems; and potassium, which keeps plants tough and disease resistant and boosts successful flowering and fruiting.

Plants constantly remove all three of these major nutrients – plus a whole series of other elements known as micronutrients – from the soil, which means you need to be just as constantly replacing them. How you do this depends on what stage of the apocalypse you're at.

Stage 1

At the start of the apocalypse, you'll have access to fertilizers looted from the garden centre. Whether granular or liquid, they're all light and easy to use, and they come with plenty of information about their NPK ratios and correct application rates. Do follow the instructions, as using too much – in

NPK isn't the acronym of an ethically dubious foreign militia but the chemical symbols for nitrogen (N), phosphorus (P) and potassium (K). We know. K, right? Why? What has the letter K got to do, in any way, with the word 'potassium'? It's stuff like this that gets people started on the whole science-is-rubbish, who-needs-vaccines, climate-change-is-just-a-leftist-conspiracy road. However: knowing the N:P:K ratio of a fertilizer helps you judge how useful it is.

particular of single-nutrient fertilizers – can actually reduce yields. Plus too much nitrogen of any kind leads to floppy, juicy growth that, as far as predators are concerned, just screams 'Eat me!'

Many of these man-made fertilizers will be quick release, meaning their NPK comes in an easily absorbable chemical form that gives plants an instant boost. They will wash out of the soil relatively fast, though. An alternative is the kind of organic fertilizers you'll have to use in stages three and four: they take longer to work but include many if not all plant micronutrients and also give beneficial soil microorganisms a boost.

Stage 2

As your supplies of shop-looted fertilizer begin to run out, you'll need to find other sources. The one closest to hand – if you'll forgive us – is urine. Yes, your own urine. Sorry, but nobody said the apocalypse would be tasteful.

All wee, including the human kind, breaks down in soil to release fantastically absorbable, heavily nitrogen-packing ammonium salts – and as the average adult pees out 11 g of nitrogen every day,[46] you can't afford to flush this valuable resource down the loo. Instead, go on the compost heap, where your nitrogen will be added to the mix. This might sound mucky, but wee is sterile when it leaves your body.

Don't pee directly on young or leafy plants, though. Not because that would be a bit Russian-call-girl-in-the-presidential-suite, but because used neat, the uric acid it contains can scorch tender roots and stems. Instead, collect wee that doesn't go on the compost heap in a bucket, then dilute its contents 1:10 with water before use.

So that's your nitrogen sorted. What about potassium? A quickly available apocalyptic replacement for manufactured potassium fertilizers is going to be ash from bonfires and wood-burning stoves. It only contains an average of 4 per cent K,[47] but that's better than no per cent K. As rain washes potassium away pretty quickly, store ash under cover, and either scatter it in small amounts directly around the base of plants or mix it in with other organic matter at mulching time.

Organic can mean three things. One, a nutrient in its elemental and not very useable chemical form, e.g. nitrogen gas. Two, a fertilizer that started life as a plant or part of an animal. And three, the kind of gardener who will defriend you if you mention pesticides.

Stage 3

As the apocalypse progresses, you'll want to start making use of well-rotted manure. Aka, poo. Yes, we're back in the whole going-to-the-toilet arena, although this time it's farm animals that are doing the business. The anus of a chicken, cow or horse is basically a geyser of black gold – grab yourself one and, as long as you leave their leavings to decompose under cover for a year, you're Daniel Day Lewis in *There Will Be Blood*. And the good news for your colleagues is that making a dung heap doesn't require you to stay in character.

Pick from the post-apocalypse poo menu, below. If there's no poo to hand (sorry), don't panic: after six months your garden compost heap will be ready. But as it doesn't have such a high NPK content as manure, use it for improving soil rather than relying on it to feed plants. And if anyone ever tells you to make a liquid fertilizer by steeping compost in water, please laugh at them: lab analysis shows that this 'compost tea' has barely any NPK content at all.[51]

Finally, a word about human manure. If you're trapped on another planet, like

HANDY TABLE NO. 9 NOT TO BE SNIFFED AT

WHAT POO IS IT?	WHAT'S ITS NPK RATIO?	WHAT'S IT MADE OF?	POO RATING	POO REVIEW
Farmyard manure[48]	3:2:4	Cow poo, cow pee, poohy straw, plus (sometimes) sheep poo		High nutrient levels, plus lots of OM too, but not so great at providing root-building phosphates
Poultry manure[49]	3:3:2	Chicken poo, pee and poohy bedding		A great all-round poo!
Horse manure[50]	2:1:2	Horse poo, pee and poohy bedding		Not as rich in nutrients as cow manure, but still handy for fruiting crops like tomatoes, squash and strawberries

Matt Damon in *The Martian*, then yes, you could use your own poo as fertilizer. But the human gut being what it is, Matt was lucky not to be infected with either *Escherichia coli*, rotavirus, norovirus, *Salmonella*, *Shigella* or *Campylobacter*, any one of which could have killed him before he was, in a highly believable scenario, catapulted back into space under a tarpaulin. So if you're staying on Earth, best not to use your own poo.

Stage 4

By now the apocalypse will be ripening into full-scale global catastrophe, and you'll want to make use of the lowest-maintenance kind of fertilizing of all: the kind where plants do the feeding for you.

You already know that green manures increase the amount of organic matter in your soil. Even better, those from the legume family can increase a soil's nitrogen levels. That's because – given the right conditions – legumes like red clover, vetch, blue lupin and field beans will develop tiny, pinkish-red bumps on their roots filled with a group of soil bacteria called rhizobia. These absorb nitrogen gas from the air and turn or 'fix' it into nitrates, which plants can then use directly.

Leguminous manures are particularly apocalypse-friendly, as in seed form they barely need any storage space, and they only take a few minutes to sow. And if you let a small area flower and set seed, you can collect and keep it for next year's sowing, rather than continuously having to source fertilizers off-site.

They're not a magic wand, though. When there's already a lot of nitrogen in the soil and/or the right kind of rhizobia aren't in residence, legumes won't form those important root nodules.[52] If you leave the plants too long and they start to flower and set seed, they'll have used any nitrogen they've fixed for their own baby-making benefit. And even if you cut the plants down at the right moment – when they've made the maximum amount of nitrogen-rich top growth but before they start diverting energy into flowering – there's no guarantee that any crop that follows immediately will yield better.[53] In fact, in very dry conditions they might actually yield less, as the manure will have sucked up valuable moisture while it was growing.[54]

Having said that, if you manure with legumes over several years and either sow them mixed with or followed by a grass-type manure such as winter rye or oats, they should eventually increase the amount of nitrogen in the soil.[55] Either way, they are cast-iron guaranteed to increase the amount of humus and soil microbes in your garden. All of this will improve its overall fertility, and your life.

Choices, choices

By now you may be feeling that a zombie garden is essentially a large toilet. Still, there are things other than faecal matter you can add to boost fertility. Blood. Bones. Rotten fish. Rotten seaweed. Before you feel too nauseous, let's sum up the whole lot in, yes, a handy table.

Humus (as opposed to houmous) is a dark, mucus-like substance that's the end product of organic matter breaking down in soil. It's crucial for soil fertility but no good with crudités.

HANDY TABLE NO. 10 FEED LINES

NUTRIENT CONTENT	PRE-APOCALYPSE	POST-APOCALYPSE[56]
Bit of everything	'All-purpose' branded fertilizers, e.g. Growmore, Miracle-Gro Potato fertilizers Pelleted chicken manure Fish, blood and bone	Composted poultry manure and bedding Composted farmyard manure and bedding
High N	Sulphate of ammonia Blood meal	Urine Leguminous green manures Hair, feathers and wool Rabbit manure
High P	Superphosphate	Ground, cooked bones Fish scraps
High K	Sulphate of potash Liquid tomato fertilizers	Comfrey/comfrey tea Wood ash Composted seaweed Composted horse manure and bedding

ZOMBIES ARE TRUE, THIS ISN'T

NO. 3 'YOU KAN GET ALL YOUR K FROM KOMFREY'

Many gardeners will tell you that comfrey – a hairy brute of a perennial, with deep taproots, a large spiralling crown of leaves and pinkish-purple bell-shaped flowers – is the Best Plant Evah for drawing potassium from deep layers of soil and storing it in its leaves. Grow enough comfrey, they say, and you can meet the K needs of your cropping plants by chopping up its leaves and laying them on the soil, adding them to your compost or steeping them in water to make a (very stinky) liquid feed called comfrey tea.

This isn't strictly true. First of all, comfrey is far from being the only plant that stores potassium in its leaves, and it isn't even the best: the leaves of horrible old stinging nettle contain almost exactly the same K concentration, while red clover shoots hold almost a third as much again.[57]

Comfrey does *have* potassium: its NPK ratio is 4:1:16,[58] and you'll find around 10 g K in the cut leaves of one mature plant. An established comfrey plant can handle being cut down twice a year without weakening it, meaning one plant can provide a potential 20 g

K a year. Meanwhile, your super-hungry veg plants will need to absorb around 30 g K per square metre every year.[59] That means in theory you should plant one and a half comfreys for each square metre of veg garden.

This seems doable until you realize that a mature comfrey plant will easily take up a whole square metre of space. In other words, to meet all your K needs with this feisty grower, you need to use 60 per cent of your site for a permanent planting of comfrey.

So by all means plant comfrey wherever you have room for it: it'll grow in shady spots that are no good for veg, and it's useful to have a lightweight, renewable source of K on-site. But you'll still have to bring in potassium from elsewhere. Which means back to wood ash and – sorry – poo and pee.

Yes, pee has potassium[60] in it too, as well as magnesium and phosphorus. Basically your bladder is like a bag of liquid Miracle-Gro with a body attached.

SKILL NO. 5
WATERING

You need to water plants. Everyone knows that! But we bet that when you start planting your zombie garden, you'll still get the watering wrong.

Here are some of the ways you can get watering wrong:

- **Not watering enough** Particularly easy to do with any plant in a container, from tiny seedlings to full-on fruit bushes. Plants transpire – lose water through their leaves – as constantly as the un-undead breathe, and on a hot day they can lose litres of water this way. In hot, dry weather, you may need to water plants in pots every day until you can see water running out of the bottom of the container.

- **Watering too much** The rule here is go moist, not wet. If soil has so much water in it that there are no pockets of air left, roots can suffocate. Don't leave seedlings or container-grown plants standing in trays of water for long periods, and don't water heavy soils at all for a few days after a good fall of rain.

- **Watering at the wrong time** Different kinds of fruit and veg need different amounts of water at different stages of growth. Some need extra water when they're starting to crop – some don't. Sigh.

- **Watering erratically** This confuses plants and makes them angry. Tomato fruit, for example, will split and/or rot at the ends if you follow a long dry period with a sudden heavy dousing. Keep the water supply slow and steady.
- **Watering in the wrong place** Roots need water. Leaves don't. Splashing water all over plants' top halves while leaving their feet dry makes plants susceptible to all sorts of nasty leaf moulds and blights. Which is why seep hoses are nearly always a better way of irrigating than sprayers and sprinklers.

This all probably seems a bit worrying. Luckily, you have Chapter 5's plant-by-plant watering advice. In the meantime, here's a useful rule of thumb: whenever soil around a plant has dried out to roughly two to three centimetres below the surface, water enough to reach the base of the root ball. Do that, and you're unlikely to actually kill anything.

Gardening books always describe the ideal growing conditions as 'moist but well drained'. Which is about as useful as saying 'wet but dry'. What they're trying to get across is that most plants like to have access to plenty of water without actively sitting in a puddle..

SKILL NO. 6
WEEDING

You're probably familiar with the phrase 'a weed is just a plant in the wrong place'.

Like a zombie is just a dead person in the wrong place. Or a hipster is just a beard in the wrong place. No. Weeds are bad, and you must get rid of all of them.

Why? Here are two reasons:

- They compete with your cropping plants for light, water and food, reducing your yields.
- They look like shit.

Both are, to our minds, perfectly valid, though in an apocalypse the first reason is the more pressing.

Weed ID

Some weeds are really easy to spot. If you can't identify a stinging nettle, for instance, then you clearly didn't spend enough of your teenage years hanging round rubbish dumps drinking WKD. However, until you get used to your site and the particular set of weeds that grow there, you might find it difficult to tell the difference between other less familiar weeds and your veg plants. Particularly when they're at the all-babies-look-the-same seedling stage.

So if you're faced with a plant you haven't seen before and aren't sure whether it's a weed, ask yourself two questions. First, is it growing exactly where you don't want it to? Second, does it spread as easily as an STI in a sixth form? If the answer to either or both of these questions is yes, then it is indeed a weed, and you need have no concerns about obliterating it.

When you first find your zombie garden site, it'll probably be full of really evil perennial weeds: dock, nettle, bramble, creeping thistle, couch grass, creeping buttercup. Don't know what any of these are? Don't worry. Spray the lot with glyphosate while repeating 'The use of chemical weedkillers is perfectly reasonable in an apocalypse.' Or – if you can afford to be patient – first cut off any flowers or seed heads and burn them. Then cover what's left with a thick layer of something light-excluding – flattened cardboard boxes weighted down with stones, an old carpet or a sheet of damp-proof membrane over a layer of

compost. After nine months to a year, the weeds will die from the lack of light, and you can dig the clean ground over, ready for planting.

Job done, you think. No. Weeds are like the far right: just when you think you've got rid of them, they rise again. But once weeds are growing among your cropping plants, you can't use chemicals or cardboard. You have to get mechanical.

The quickest, easiest way to do this is to use a hoe to cut weeds down at the seedling stage. Stick the sharp edge of the hoe just under the soil surface, then push and pull it quickly backwards and forwards so it cuts the tops away from their roots. (Go carefully, or you'll also slice up the veg plants.) Try to hoe on dry days so that you can leave the decapitated weeds on the soil to shrivel; in warm, wet weather you'll have to spend extra time raking them up, or you can bet any with roots still attached will spring back to life.

Hoe often – as often as every ten days in peak growing season – because once weeds in veg rows get too big and settled in, you have to get down on your knees and fork them out by hand. This is incredibly boring.

ZOMBIES ARE TRUE, THIS ISN'T

NO. 4 'IF YOU MULCH, YOU DON'T HAVE TO WEED'

Mulch is excellent. It helps stop soil washing away, keeps temperatures steady and reduces water loss. Plus worms slowly drag it down into the soil as it rots, improving OM levels.

But the thing mulch doesn't do, no matter what gardening books say, is stop you having to weed. If mulch is upwards of five centimetres thick, it will smother any annual seedlings that germinate in the soil below. But it won't stop relentless perennials like dock or bramble nosing through: they laugh in the face of ten centimetres, never mind five, and the only way to get rid of them is to dig them out.

Also, weed seeds are first-class travellers, masters of transporting themselves about on the wind, in bird poo or even on the feet of animals or marauding zombies. Loose, moist and warm, mulch can make pretty much the perfect seedbed. The minute seeds land, they will literally start putting down roots. At the right time of year, seeds can sprout in mulch as thickly as cress.

So by all means mulch. But be prepared to dig out perennial weeds first, and keep your hoe well sharpened.

SKILL NO. 7
COLLECTING SEED

You'll remember in Chapter 1 we said that as soon as the apocalypse begins you need to grab as many varieties of veg seed as you can. That's all good. But after the first season's growing, when your seed packets will either be empty or past their use-by dates and the garden centres will have been picked clean by looters, you'll need to rely on creating your own supplies.

Luckily nearly all the plants in a zombie garden will, if you give them a chance, first flower, then create – or 'set' – their own seed. Broccoli, for example: the bit you eat, the floret, is actually an immature flower head. Beans and peas are just edible pods and seeds – let some mature and you can sow them the next year. Onions and carrots left in the ground will, in their second year, throw up flower heads that produce literally thousands of seeds.

So, leaving plants to set seed is easy enough. But the seeds themselves will be only worth saving if they come from what's known as an open-pollinated (OP) variety. OP plant varieties are always homozygous. That means their seed will grow into plants that look, crop and taste exactly the same as themselves.

Unless, that is, they are cross-pollinated by different varieties you're growing nearby, either other OPs or, despite our instructions in Chapter 1, F1 hybrids. In which case, you've effectively bred your own kind of vegetable and there's no knowing what the outcome will be. It could be a tomato that, when you slice it open, contains the face of Jesus. Or it could just taste really, really bad. To avoid either, it's safest to let just one variety of a vegetable flower at a time. And then, for maximum gene-pool health, save seed from at least ten –

> Homozygous **means that a plant's parents had identical genes. Couples that wear identical clothes are not homozygous; they're just annoying.**

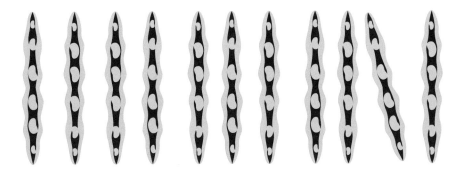

preferably more – of the sturdiest, most vigorous plants.

When to collect

Like so much about zombie gardening, timing is important. You don't want to take seed before it's fully developed, or it may not germinate. Leave it too long after it's ripened, though, and the seeds will suddenly all disappear: pods split, the wind blows, fruit gets eaten and zombie gardeners go hungry the following year.

As usual, different rules apply to different plants, but here are some general guidelines.

The kind of seed that is inside a fruit – like tomatoes or squash – will be fully developed by the time the fruit is ripe, so just set aside a few undamaged fruits at harvest time and scoop out the seeds inside.

For pod bearers like peas and beans, wait until the pods have turned brown and dry and rattle when you shake them.

To collect the seeds, crack open the casing and shake or scrape them out.

Seed that sets in heads at the top of flower stalks, like kale or beetroot, is particularly prone to suddenly disappearing. Either check for ripeness every day or, as heads begin to ripen – usually from the bottom up – tie paper bags around them with twine or elastic bands. That way the seeds drop into the bags as they ripen, and you can have an actual life.

Storing

Damp seed goes mouldy and won't germinate, so once you've gathered your seed, spread it out somewhere airy for a week or so to make sure it's properly dry. Gunk-covered seeds like the ones inside tomatoes and pumpkins benefit from first being stirred into a jug of water then left for forty-eight hours to help separate them from their coating.

To be sure you get maximum ger-mination rates out of your seed, you next have to separate it from all the little bits of cohabiting non-seed crap, known as chaff. Start by grinding seed heads through a sieve: garden sieves, the large-holed kind you use for sifting compost, are fine for large seeds, but kitchen sieves work better for very fine seed. This will break up and get rid of quite a bit of chaff. But to finish the cleaning process properly, you'll need to winnow.

From the Old English for 'wind', winnowing traditionally involved going outside on a breezy day and tipping the seed/chaff mix backwards and forwards from one shallow basket into another. The wind would blow away the much lighter chaff, while the seed fell into the basket.

What, we wonder, is the Old English for 'cock-up'? Because unless you grew up hand-winnowing rice on a paddy in Malaysia, what actually happens is that the wind either gusts or drops, you misjudge the distances and your seed ends up all over the floor. As you learnt from the bread-making prep on page 97, before the apocalypse an electric fan made winnowing easier, but that's now off the menu. And unfortunately, antique hand-operated winnowing machines will be hard to source for anyone not living next door to an agricultural museum. So be prepared for winnowing to take time.

Once you finally manage to get them clean, you can put your seeds away for the winter – though not anywhere airtight, as they're alive and need to breathe. Storing them in labelled paper bags or envelopes in an old drawer or wooden box is fine, particularly if you can keep it out of the reach of mice.

You won't be able to rely on refrigeration to keep seeds fresh, so concentrate instead on keeping them as cool and dry as possible. A shed or garage will do, but as it's likely to get quite damp, see if you can track down any of those little packets of silica gel that were always at the bottom of pre-apocalypse packaging. Popped into the same container as the seeds, they'll absorb moisture from the air and reduce the danger of your seed going mouldy before it gets the chance to feed you next year.

How long your seed will stay usable for depends on what kind it is: seed from brassicas (like kale, cabbage or broccoli) will last for up to four years, but parsnip seed will be rubbish after just a year. The rule of thumb, though, is that the fresher the seed, the better the germination rate, so it's worth collecting seed from at least some of your veg every year.

American homesteaders go one better: they clean their seed using sets of stacking wooden sieves with different grades of metal mesh on their bottoms. The trays' bottoms, not the Americans'.

SKILL NO. 8
ROTATION

Unless the apocalypse only lasts a year, you're going to need to rotate your crops. This doesn't involve standing them on some kind of giant lazy Susan. Instead it means growing plants from the same or closely related biological families in a different patch of ground every year for at least three years.

Because there are quite a few families in a zombie garden, rotation requires pencil, paper and a reasonable head for math to organize. So why would you bother?

First, it helps stop crop-specific pests and diseases building up in any particular patch. Just as importantly, it makes the most of scarce resources – putting nitrogen-fixing beans, for example, into exhausted soil just vacated by potatoes or onions saves on the amount of fertilizing you need to do. Also, gardeners have traditionally and rather cleverly boiled down all the many veg-garden families into just four simple groups, each of which has similar likes and dislikes. Which means it's time for, hooray, another handy table.

HANDY TABLE NO. 11 ROTARY SOCIETIES

ROTATION GROUP	VEG	LIKES
Brassicas	Cabbage Calabrese Broccoli Kale Turnip	Alkaline pH High N levels
Solanums	Potatoes Tomatoes	Acid pH High N levels
Legumes	Broad beans French beans Runner beans Leguminous green manures e.g. clover	Low N levels
Roots and alliums	Carrots Parsnips Onions Spring onions	Low N levels

HANDY TABLE NO. 12 A NICE, SIMPLE FOUR-YEAR PLAN FOR A SINGLE BED

YEAR 1: SOLANUMS	YEAR 2: ROOTS	YEAR 3: LEGUMES	YEAR 4: BRASSICAS
Potatoes	Onions and garlic	Broad beans	Sprouting broccoli
Tomatoes	Carrots	French beans	Cabbage
	Parsnips	Runner beans	Turnip
		Peas	Kale

Rotation always follows a specific order – just like certain memorable cultural figures:

■ John is followed by Paul is followed by George is followed by Ringo
■ Kourtney is followed by Kim is followed by Khloe is followed by Caitlyn
■ Solanums are followed by roots are followed by legumes are followed by brassicas

To show you how rotation works, we've created Handy Table No. 12 (above), a nice, simple four-year plan for a single bed or other area in your zombie garden. Although after reading it, sharp-eyed readers will be wondering: *What happened to all the other annual zombie-garden crops, like squash and beetroot? When do I get to grow the green manure you keep banging on about?*

The answer to a) is that while you should still grow them on a different patch of ground each year, these kinds of veg count as neutral: you can grow them alongside legumes, roots, brassicas or solanums without any trouble. As for b), green manure is sometimes a legume, sometimes not; some you grow in winter, some in spring or summer. So you can fit them into a rotation in lots of different ways.

Before you give up and decide that starving might be preferable to working all this stuff out, take a look at Handy Table No. 13 on the right. If Handy Table No. 12 was good, this is even better, because it suggests a way to plant that takes into account growing seasons, nutritional needs and pH preferences, and has more stuff to eat.

This is just a suggestion – you'll need to experiment to find out what works best for you, depending on what you grow, what kind of soil you have, and how you've divided up your plot. Don't

HANDY TABLE NO. 13

A SLIGHTLY MORE COMPLICATED BUT STILL REALLY USEFUL FOUR-YEAR PLAN

YEAR 1	MANURE	YEAR 2	MANURE	YEAR 3	MANURE	YEAR 4	MANURE
Potatoes	Winter rye	Onions and garlic	Phacelia	Broad beans	Clover/ ryegrass mix	Sprouting broccoli	Farmyard or poultry manure
Tomatoes		Carrots		French beans	Wood ash	Cabbage	
Pumpkin		Parsnips		Runner beans		Turnips	
Squash		Beetroot		Peas		Kale	
Courgettes		Chard		Amaranth			
Will benefit from high N and K and low pH	Protects soil over winter, adds OM	Will benefit from post-potato low N	Increases N and OM	Will benefit from post-phacelia high OM	Increases N and K and raises pH	Will benefit from post-clover and ash high N and pH	Lowers pH, raises N, P and K

despair, though. Rotation might at first seem complicated, but in fact it's more like the Spider-Man movies: you wait a few years, then just repeat everything all over again.

Let battle commence

Well done! You've now learned all the basic skills necessary to sow, grow and get the best out of any patch of ground the apocalypse throws at you. That means it's time for us to introduce you, in person and in some really fine detail, to the plants you're going to grow.

But before we do that, let's take a moment to see what use your zombie survivor group could make of what is, for now, the world's most abundant resource: zombies.

DEAD COOL

FIVE USES FOR THE GARDEN ZOMBIE

Don't want to waste the apocalypse's biggest crop? Here's what to do!

Meat compost

After repelling an attack on your compound, bury the resulting glut of zombie corpses in one-metre-deep trenches in a quiet part of your garden. Leave them undisturbed for at least two years, by which time their flesh will have rotted and released its nutrients, any dangerous microorganisms such as *E. coli* or zombie-virus will have died[62] and the now nicely enriched ground should be safe to plant in.

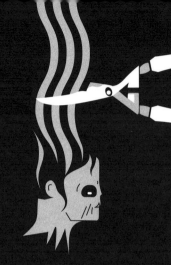

Hairy scary

After decapitating a zombie, be sure to cut off its hair and put it on your compost heap, where it will add slow-release nitrogen as it rots. Or, where deer and rabbits are a problem, stuff the hair into old pairs of tights. Hung around the perimeter, the smell will make grazing animals think your garden is guarded by predators and/or stocking fetishists. Either of which is pretty off-putting.

Bone up

Throw unwanted zombies onto the bonfire to burn off their flesh and sterilize their skeletons. Then smash the now dry and brittle bones into little bits with a lump hammer before digging the resulting bonemeal into the soil. This is a good way both to raise phosphorus levels and to work out all the inevitable frustrations of living in an apocalypse.

Scarecrowing

For a scarecrow that actually works, attach a captured zombie by a long chain to a post in your garden and let it roam about. While birds will soon work out that a broom handle with a hat on it isn't any kind of a threat, a zombie dressed as Worzel Gummidge will really put the wind up them.

Alternative oxen

Hitch a brace of zombies to old farming equipment and use them in place of draught animals for ploughing, harrowing and sowing crops on open ground.

NB: To get them moving, walk a little way in front – they don't respond to the phrase 'giddy-up'.

SQUARE-METRE STIR-FRY

Now you know a little more about vegetable families
and how to rotate crops, it's time to put this knowledge
to some use and grow yourself an actual meal.
You won't need an allotment with acres of beds
to do it in either.

Because the good news about this prep is that the only space you need is one square metre of soil. And that could be a section of open ground in a back garden, or just a series of pots.

It may not sound like much, but one square metre is enough space to provide all the vegetables you need for a healthy, nutrient-rich stir-fry of carrots, mangetout, courgettes, spring onions and cabbage.

Even better, using your new skill of rotation you can grow the same vegetables on your plot year after year, without pests and diseases building up, or particular micronutrients getting exhausted.

Here's how.

1 SOURCE YOUR PLANTS

You could buy young plug plants from garden centres or catalogues, then plant them straight into your plot, but we'd suggest you sow everything yourself. Yes, it takes a little more effort, but you'll be building crucial apocalypse-surviving experience.

This is what you'll need:

- **One packet courgette seed** – preferably a compact bush-type variety, as then you don't have to train it up something vertical
- **One packet spring onion seed**
- **One packet carrot seed** – choose a summer-cropping variety
- **One packet mangetout pea seed**
- **One packet white or green ballhead-type cabbage seed** – check the packet to make sure it's a summer-cropping variety
- **One small bag seed compost**
- **Two 5 cm module trays and three 9 cm pots** or six small yoghurt pots with drainage holes and fifteen cardboard loo-roll tubes
- **One twenty-five-litre bag of composted farmyard manure** or a packet of all-purpose granular fertilizer
- **One square metre of weed-free soil**, either in open ground, a raised bed or containers (at least three of these should be 40 cm deep or more)

2 PREPARE THE GROUND

Before you start sowing, divide your growing area into quarters, so that you have four spaces each with a soil area of roughly a quarter of a square metre. Each of these quarters will hold plants from a different rotation group:

- Courgettes (from the go-anywhere neutral group)
- Carrots and spring onions (from the roots and alliums group)
- Mangetout (from the legumes group)
- Cabbage (from the brassicas group)

Spread a 2.5 cm layer of the well-rotted manure over the soil everywhere except the roots and alliums patch, as onions don't yield as well when there's loads of nitrogen available. Or, if you're not using manure, apply granular fertilizer at planting-out time.

Growing in pots? Work out soil area by casting your mind back to Year 9 and the nice maths teacher writing 'Today's activity: πr^2!' on the interactive whiteboard. That was when you learnt to find the area of a circle by multiplying the radius by itself, then multiplying the result by 3.14. Before setting fire to the lockers at the back of the classroom and making the nice maths teacher cry.

3 SOW YOUR CABBAGE

You're aiming to end up with two cabbages, so to allow for pests, diseases and other disasters, sow at least six cabbage seeds, ideally in early February. Fill three of the modules in your trays, or three yoghurt pots, with moist seed compost. Sow two seeds to a module or pot, 2 cm deep. Cover with a plastic bag, and keep at or above 7–10° C until germination. Within fourteen days you should see seedlings: gently tug out the weaker seedling in each module or pot (this is known as 'thinning out') and put the survivors somewhere cool and bright while they develop. Start to harden the young plants off once they're 15 cm high.

4 START THE SPRING ONIONS

Early in March, take the other module tray, or three more yoghurt pots, and sow the spring onion seed. You're aiming to end up with twenty plants, so sow ten seeds to a module or pot, 1 cm deep. Cover with a plastic bag and keep at 10–20° C until germination – up to twenty-one days – then grow somewhere cool and bright for a couple of weeks before hardening off.

Towards the end of the month, as the soil begins to warm up, plant out two cabbage plants, 40 cm apart, in the brassica section of your patch. Water in thoroughly, protect with brassica collars and insect mesh and begin slug patrol.

5 PLANT THEM OUT, START THE CARROTS

By early April the soil should be warming and drying out nicely after winter. Now's the moment to rake the roots-and-alliums area back and forth until you've made a fine tilth. Then plant out two of your modules of onions, without separating the individual plants, so that the clumps are roughly 25 cm apart. Water in gently. Keep killing those slugs.

In the middle of the month (as long as the weather isn't either very cold or very wet) sow the carrot seed directly into the roots-and-alliums area: draw out a shallow trench 1.5 cm deep, 15 cm away from the onions and, if the soil is dry, water it gently with a fine rose. Sow a seed every centimetre or so, then rake soil back over down the row. Keep moist but not wet until germination (seven to twenty-one days). A month after sowing, thin to one plant every 5–10 cm, depending on the size of the variety you're using, and protect with insect mesh.

6 SOW THE MANGETOUT

In early May, fill three 9 cm pots or fifteen loo-roll tubes with seed compost (stand the tubes on a tray and tie them with string to stop them falling over). You want to end up with ten mangetout, so sow either five seeds to a pot or one to a tube, 5 cm deep. Germinate them at 10–24° C, taking anti-mouse precautions if necessary, and grow on somewhere cool and bright until shoots are about 7.5 cm high.

In late May, plant the mangetout in Legume Corner. Build a tripod of sticks or bamboo canes for them to climb up, and site one plant at the base of each stick, watering in well. Surround plants with twigs to stop pigeons pecking off the tops; remain on slug alert.

7 START THE COURGETTES

As soon as the mangetout are planted, sow your courgettes. You'll only need one plant, so fill two 9 cm pots with moist seed compost and sow one seed per pot, 2 cm deep, standing the seed on its thin edge so it doesn't rot. Cover them with plastic bags and keep at a steady 21° C or more until germination, in around a week's time. Grow on somewhere warm and bright – under a cloche outside would be ideal – until their third jagged leaves appear. Then harden off.

8 PLANT THE COURGETTE

In late June, it'll be time to plant out the courgette: just one, bang in the middle of your neutral area. Water it in well. If it succumbs to slug attack, use your second courgette as a replacement.

By July, slugs will have learnt to fear your name, and all your crops will be in full harvest mode. Slosh some oil in the wok, give yourself a pat on the back and get cooking.

9 WHAT ABOUT NEXT YEAR?

The following spring, proceed exactly as before. But this time, rotate how you sow each of your quarters one step through the 'neutral – roots and alliums – legumes – brassicas' cycle. In other words, last year's courgette corner becomes this year's carrots-and-onions spot; last year's carrots-and-onions becomes this year's mangetout, etc., etc. As long as you add some manure every year, you can keep this up almost indefinitely. Or at least until the apocalypse gets started. ✳

5

THE GROUNDWORK

One thing nobody tells you when you start growing food is just how different plants are. The basics of sowing and growing that we discussed in Chapter 3 are always pretty much the same, but it's knowing the little details about what each plant likes and dislikes that makes a zombie garden productive.

Not knowing those details means your seeds might not germinate, your plants might get sick and your crop might not develop properly. That could mean the difference between survival and starvation.

Also, every zombie garden site is different. When you're planning what to plant in a survival situation, you need to assess which crops are easiest to grow in your specific set of conditions. Then you have to work out which will provide the highest quantity of calories and other nutrients.

You need to assess which crops are easiest to grow in your conditions

So in this chapter, we get right down to earth, giving you the specific information you need to grow twenty key varieties of zombie-garden plant. We'll tell you how many of the most vital nutrients a single plant can provide and how long it can support a single survivor. We'll show when you can expect to tuck in to a particular crop and how much of the year it'll feed you for. We'll look at how to harvest each crop, how to deal with its most common enemies and how well it will do in containers. Finally, we'll give you a month-by-month growing calendar that will show you what to plant to stay alive, whatever time of year the zombies begin to bite.

GROWERS' NOTES

To save you time, we'll deal with plants in order of their nutritional usefulness – which means starting with the spuds. But before we do, here's a few things to be aware of.

All the plants in this chapter will grow best in soil that never dries out completely and drains well in wet weather – but we've marked those which are able to cope with particularly wet or particularly dry conditions. All will enjoy a soil pH of 6.5–7, unless marked otherwise. Most will do well if you add well-rotted compost or green manure to their growing site, but we've pointed out plants that need particularly rich soils and those that yield better when they're kept hungry.

All like plenty of light, but we've marked those that can't deal with any shade, as well as those that will put up with shade for part of the day. The temperature range we give for seed germination refers to soil temperature, which in spring and summer is a few degrees lower than the air temperature. Test open ground with a soil thermometer or use Handy Table No. 7 (see page 104) to check what under-cover options will provide the right temperature.

As well as giving traditional line-'em-up-in-a-row planting distances, we recommend how many plants to grow in a square metre. This should help you work out how much food your site can provide.

To make seed-saving easier, any varieties we've recommended are open pollinated (OP) unless otherwise stated.

For anyone using containers, remember your plants will need more watering and feeding than if you were planting them in open ground. Not all veg cope with pots, but wherever possible we've suggested a few named varieties that usually do well where space is limited. We've also given you a guide to what depth of container to use.

Where we recommend feeding with all-purpose, high-N or high-K fertilizers, check Handy Table No. 10 (see page 116) for which fertilizer options will fit the bill.

To keep things simple, the survivor-day figures assume you're meeting all your daily needs from just one kind of vegetable. Which of course you don't – so hooray, you don't have to fill every inch of your zombie garden with only one kind of veg.

KEY

 Copes with wetter conditions

 Copes with drier conditions

 Does best at pH 7–7.5

 Does best at pH 5.5–6

 Must have full sun

 Copes with partial shade

 Copes well with light, sandy soils

 Copes well with heavy clay soils

 Add lots of manure

 Don't add manure

 Must have deep soil

 Copes with shallow soil

 Not for windy sites

 OK on windy sites

POTATOES
Solanum tuberosum

The main thing to know about potatoes is this: to crop well, tubers need cool, moist and dark conditions, and they must be at least 15 cm below the soil surface. Too hot or too dry a soil and though the foliage above ground may look great, the spuds themselves will hardly develop. And if the soil is so shallow that light gets to the tubers, they turn green and poisonous.

This is why one of the most useful things you do when growing potatoes is mound soil and/or mulch over their leafy tops – known as 'earthing up'. To novice zombie gardeners, this feels counterintuitive. Why would you stop the plant from being able to photosynthesize? Because beneath every potato leaf is a bud with the potential to develop into a stolon. This is a special kind of stem that grows underground and bears tubers at its end. So what you're actually doing when you earth up is giving the plant the opportunity to make more stolons. And hence give you a bigger crop.

Potato varieties are divided into three groups, which each need progressively longer to crop: tiny first earlies (aka new potatoes), less tiny second earlies, and the big fat maincrop. Plant them all at the same time: once your soil has warmed to 7° C or above, in rows of holes 10 cm deep, 45 cm apart in all directions. Drop one tuber into each hole, backfill gently and, if frost seems likely, cover with fleece or a mulch of leaf mould.

Now wait. After two to four weeks, you'll start to see green shoots. Once these are 10 cm high (or before, if frost seems likely) earth up: dig out some of the soil from either side of your rows, throw in some compost or well-rotted manure and use this to mound a ridge 5–10 cm high over the shoots. As the shoots grow, top up with more earth or a mulch that blocks light but isn't attractive to slugs: leaf mould is ideal. Continue to earth up using soil and mulch, or mulch alone, until the ridge is about 20 cm above the original surface level, then leave the shoots to grow on until harvest time.

HOW TO GROW POTATOES

How many? Three plants will provide two survivor-days of calories[63]

On the table Midsummer to midwinter

Rotation group Solanums

Plants per m² Four

Chitting Between mid-February and mid-March, choose healthy, hen-egg-sized tubers and stand them, laid out on trays or in old egg cartons, with their eyes (the little white protuberances at one end) pointing upwards. Leave them somewhere cool, bright and frost free for four to six weeks, by which time they should have developed the sturdy pink-and-white shoots that mean they are ready to plant out, as described on the left.

Feeding Use an all-purpose fertilizer at planting. Use a high-N fertilizer at first earthing up.

Watering Water well whenever the soil dries out 7.5 cm below the surface.

Harvesting For first earlies, harvest fourteen weeks after planting. For second earlies and maincrop varieties, start when the leaves begin to yellow from the top down. In all cases, wait for a dry day, then dig the prongs of a fork into the soil about a foot away from each plant and gently lever out the tubers. Leave them somewhere dry so the skins can harden – ideally for two days – then store.

Main enemies **Slugs** will eat tubers, so harvest as soon as possible. **Potato cyst eelworm** attack causes leaves of odd plants in a row to yellow and dry from the ground up. Once eelworm is established, you'll have to plant spuds elsewhere. **Wireworms** nip off seedlings at the root – avoid them by not planting spuds in grassy areas. **Blight** spores cause small yellow blotches to appear on leaves, usually after forty-eight hours of warm, wet weather. The spots turn black, spread shockingly quickly and rot the tubers. There's no remedy: dig out the whole lot immediately and burn.

Pot-ability Most potato varieties will crop fine in cool, well-drained containers 45+ cm deep, but first earlies are often the most successful, as they're less likely to overheat in high summer. Whichever variety you use, have a look at the Prep for the Pre-Apocalypse on page 192, as this will give you blow-by-blow advice on how to get a good potato crop in containers.

RUNNER BEANS
Phaseolus coccineus

Runner beans are incredible climbers. After a few weeks' sulking at planting-out time, they suddenly take off and will easily grow to three metres high by midsummer. So their big ask is support.

Traditionally they're grown on either side of an A-frame of tall bamboo canes or hazel rods tied to crossbars, but you can just as easily grow them up trellises, wire fences, or arches – anything sturdy enough not to fall over when loaded with bean plant and/or pushed by a zombie.

Runners can be reluctant to start climbing, so for the first few weeks give them a helping hand by twisting the tips of stems clockwise around the supports or tying them gently into place with twine. In a good year they'll soon be covered by scarlet, pea-like flowers, followed by an abundance of dangling bunches of flat, slightly ridged green pods that make you feel like a seriously successful gardener. But then some years, for no apparent reason: nothing. Nada. No flowers, no pods. This is called not setting. White-flowered varieties like 'Czar' seem less prone to this, and they produce white beans that are good for drying. But if you are growing scarlet runners, nip off the tip of the leading shoot between your fingernails when it's reached 15 cm. This will encourage the growth of more side shoots, which set flowers and pods more reliably.

Sowing runners twice, once in April and again in July, will keep fresh pods coming until October – although the last ones probably won't ripen into dryable beans.

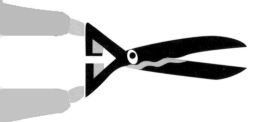

HOW TO GROW RUNNER BEANS

How many?	Two plants will provide dried beans for one survivor-day of protein[65]
On the table	Fresh, summer/autumn; dried, year round
Rotation group	Legumes
Plants per m²	Twelve
Sowing	In April, one or two beans to a 10 cm pot, 5 cm deep. Keep at 18° C until germination (which should take between seven and ten days), then grow on somewhere cool and bright. Once plants are between 7.5 and 10 cm high – and/or the frosts have finished – harden off for a week or two, then plant out at the base of your support, with 15 cm between each bean plant. Plant another row on the other side of the support, leaving roughly 60 cm between the two rows.
Feeding	Add an all-purpose fertilizer at planting out. Don't go N crazy, though – it's flowers you want, not leaves.
Watering	Runners are thirsty, particularly once they start to make flower buds. From then on until the beans are good and ripe, they'll need plenty of moisture in the soil. So after a few days without rain, give them a drink – roughly one can of water for every fourteen plants.
Harvesting	Pods are edible (and delicious) as soon as they're a few centimetres long, and if you pick every few days, starting at the bottom of the plant, more will set farther up. They're still good to eat – if stringier – up to 20 cm in length. After that, they're best for dried beans: leave pods on the plant until they begin to go yellow, then pick and leave them somewhere airy to finish drying. Once they're properly brown and wrinkly, split to get at the beans inside. Dry these on racks for a further few days, then keep in jars for up to three years.
Main enemies	**Slugs** are a menace until young plants are 30 cm high. **Birds** can also cause damage at planting time, so protect youngsters with twigs, fleece or net. If **black aphids** infest growing tips, wipe them off by hand or spray with a solution of soapy water. **Stem and root rots** are caused by various fungi, which make the bases of stems go blackish and make the tops yellow and die – pull affected plants up and burn them.
Pot-ability	Full-size varieties like 'Enorma Elite' and 'Czar' are top-heavy and greedy, so you might do better with a dwarf-type such as 'Hestia'. Either way, use a wide container at least 30 cm deep, sited somewhere sheltered but sunny. Give plants a strong support to climb up and feed weekly with a liquid high-K fertilizer.

KALE
Brassica oleracea

Kale is just fabulous. Unlike its close relative cauliflower, it grows and crops well without needing half a swimming pool of water applied every ten minutes.

As long as it's not in ground that gets waterlogged in winter, it will hold its leaves throughout the coldest time of the year, providing your group with vital vitamin C along with masses of potassium. But unlike another close relative, winter-cropping Brussels sprouts, it actually tastes good.

Because kale can get tall and top-heavy, it's best grown on firm soil. If yours is very light and sandy, tread the ground down a bit before planting out, and pile earth around stems for extra support as they get bigger. On any site, don't be afraid to prop up plants with canes if bad weather is on the way. Other than that, it's all about the protecting. Like other brassicas, kale is high on many pests' favoured-snack lists, so familiarize yourself with the Enemies list on the right and use collars, insect mesh and bird net to keep your babies safe.

HOW TO GROW KALE

How many?	One plant provides leaves for ten survivor-days of vitamin C
On the table	Autumn through to mid-May
Rotation group	Brassicas
Plants per m²	Six
Sowing	In April, in 2.5 cm module trays, two or three seeds to a module, 2.5 cm deep. Cover with plastic lids or bags and keep above 7° C until germination (seven to ten days), then chuck out the weaker seedlings to leave one in each module. Prick these out into 5 cm pots at the two-true-leaves stage, and keep them somewhere cool and bright until they have at least four true leaves – usually around six weeks after sowing. Harden off for ten to fourteen days, then plant out 50 cm apart in every direction.
Feeding	Use an all-purpose fertilizer at planting out. Use a liquid high-N fertilizer once in late summer if the leaves look a bit tired and yellow.
Watering	Keep moist until the plants are about 60 cm high, then only water in dry spells. Don't water at all in winter.
Harvesting	In late September, pick some of youngest leaves from the tip of the plant. Then pick larger leaves from lower down as you need them. In spring, side shoots will start to grow: harvest these until March.
Main enemies	**Club root** causes bulbous root swellings that kill all brassicas. It's commonest in acid soils, so raise pH above 6.8 by adding lime or wood ash two months before planting. Stop **cabbage root fly** by laying a small cardboard circle (a 'brassica collar') around each stem at planting-out time. Cover rows with cloche hoops and insect mesh straight after planting to foil the **cabbage white butterfly** and its munchy caterpillars. In autumn, replace the mesh with bird net to stop **pigeons** chowing down through the winter. Also, **slugs** will decimate young plants – but you knew that, right?
Pot-ability	'Dwarf Green Curled' and dark-leaved 'Nero di Toscana' are both widely available and do well in containers 25+ cm deep. Protect as for open ground, and give a dose of high-N fertilizer once in early summer.

BROAD BEANS
Vicia faba var. *major*

Sturdy-looking, not afraid of a bit of cold and damp and going to pieces in very hot weather, broad beans are a highly British crop.

They don't yield as heavily as runners, and unlike French beans you don't eat the whole pod, just the fat, pale-green beans nestled inside. But fresh or dried, they pack lots of protein for their weight. And even more importantly for the zombie gardener, they can be ready to harvest in late spring – a real bonus when winter stores are low and not much else is ready to eat.

The trick is to get that harvest as early as possible. If your soil isn't too clay-heavy (and therefore cold) you can sow what are known as overwintering varieties such as 'Aquadulce Claudia' direct in late October. If the winter weather hasn't been too fierce, these should start cropping in late May. Otherwise, sow in modules in late winter, aiming to plant out, with a bit of frost and wind protection, from mid-March; these plants should begin cropping in June.

The wind thing is important, by the way. Even dwarf varieties of broad bean get very top-heavy, and their stalks can snap in bad weather, finishing off your crop. So either support them with tall twiggy branches pushed into the soil all around them or make horizontal squares of twine, wound round strong stakes at a height of about 30 cm, that they can grow up through.

HOW TO GROW BROAD BEANS

How many?	Four plants will provide beans for one survivor-day of protein[65]
On the table	Fresh, late spring to late summer; dried, year round
Rotation group	Legumes
Plants per m²	Fifteen
Sowing	For an early crop, sow in January to March, in 7.5 cm pots, one to a pot, 6 cm deep. To prevent the seeds from rotting before they germinate, stand them in the soil upright rather than lying on their sides. Keep moist at 12°C until germination (seven to fourteen days), then grow on somewhere bright and cool. Around two weeks after germination, harden off for ten days. Plant out 20 cm apart in two lines, with 20 cm between the lines – this is known as a double row – and then leave 40–60 cm between that and the next double row. To keep supplies coming through summer, sow again whenever the previous batch has reached 15 cm high.
Feeding	As long as soil has plenty of OM, don't bother.
Watering	Don't let them dry out when flower buds are forming or pods setting.
Harvesting	Begin picking once pods at the bottom of the plant are about 12–15 cm long. Pick regularly, working up the plant, to maximize yield. From August on, leave pods on the plant until they blacken. Remove the beans inside, let them dry somewhere airy until their skins are fully hard, then store.
Main enemies	**Blackfly** often infest growing tips from May on: once the first set of flowers is forming pods, pinch off the main shoot about 7.5 cm down, as it's this bit they like best. **Mice** will dig up seeds: lay traps or hang module trays somewhere high and unclimbable.
Pot-ability	These are plants with chunky root systems, so really tall varieties can struggle. Try 'Aquadulce Longpod' if you have pots more than 25 cm deep; if not, a shorter variety like 'de Monica' should work well.

To get really, really early crops, sow directly into the ground in October, 10 centimetres apart, in trenches 6 centimetres deep and 20 centimetres apart. Cover the rows with a topping of 2.5 centimetres of OM and protect with cloche hoops. Once the worst of the winter is over thin to 20 centimetres apart.

AMARANTH
Amaranthus cruentus/
Amaranthus caudatus

Tall, leafy, with fluffy tassels of flowers, amaranth is a plant that should have more friends. A staple part of the Aztec diet (until they suffered their own Spanish-powered apocalypse), amaranth's vitamin-packed leaves cook like spinach, but without all the fussing over that spinach needs.

Better, its protein-rich, quinoa-like seeds – which you either pop over heat like corn or boil in water and use as an ingredient in salads, risottos, breads and biscuits – contain the amino acid lysine, making amaranth one of the most complete vegetable proteins around.[67] Unless the climate changes so much we can start large-scale growing of soya beans, anyone surviving the apocalypse in the UK should be all over amaranth.

There are two kinds to know about: *Amaranthus cruentus*, which has fairly upright flower tassels and is the type more usually grown as a leaf crop, and *A. caudatus* (aka love-lies-bleeding), which makes droopy, seedy cat's tails of flower. Both like heat but don't need it, and they are the least demanding of annuals: as long as the soil is warm and not soggy, they grow like billy from June, set flower in August and go to seed by mid-autumn. All of this makes them perfect for keeping the nutrition coming from space just vacated by broad beans or early potatoes.

Amaranth should germinate well if you rake it into fine-tilth soil outside in late June. But see how we said 'should'? For a guaranteed harvest, have some module-grown plants as back-up. After you've planted out and harvested these, keep the bed free of weeds until late the following June: amaranth self-seeds pretty easily, so you should then find lots of seedlings popping up. Once they're 10 cm high, transfer these to a new bed to grow on.

HOW TO GROW AMARANTH

How many? Fifteen plants will provide leaves and seeds for one day's protein + nine days' iron + thirty days' vitamin C + 112 days' vitamin A[67]

On the table Leaves, July to October; seeds, October to January

Rotation group Neutral

Plants per m² Fifteen

Sowing In April or early May, in 5 cm module trays, three or four seeds to a module. Scatter seed on the surface of damp compost and cover with a fine dusting of more compost. Cover with glass or a plastic bag and keep at 18° C until germination (seven to twenty days). Thin to one seedling per module, prick out ASAP (they grow fast) into 7.5 cm pots and grow on somewhere warm and bright. Harden off, then plant out in June. For the heaviest leaf crops, plant 15 cm apart in rows 30 cm apart; for maximum seed yields, plant 30 cm apart in all directions.

Feeding Though they respond to feeding, amaranths don't need rich soils – save your fertilizer for hungrier plants.

Watering Only during long dry spells.

Harvesting Either pinch off the leading shoot a few weeks after planting out to encourage leafy side shoots, and start to harvest leaves when plants are 25 cm high. Or leave the plants be until the flower tassels are just beginning to turn brownish at the tips and tiny reddish-brown seeds fall out when you shake them. Grind the flower heads through a sieve to remove the seed, then winnow before you store it. Kept in airtight containers somewhere cool, it should last for four to six months.

Main enemies **Powdery mildew** is most often a problem when the soil is dry but the air is humid, so water plants well if the weather dampens after a long dry spell.

Pot-ability *A. cruentus* varieties such as 'Kerala Red' or 'Red Garnet' work well for a crop of leaves: sow seed direct in pots 20 cm deep and harvest a few leaves per plant every three weeks.

FRENCH BEANS
Phaseolus vulgaris

Like Jason Bourne, French beans have many aliases. Cannellini, snap, flageolet, navy, borlotti, haricot, cranberry, whatever – they're all versions of *P. vulgaris*. These first produce long, smooth pods for eating fresh, then fill them with seeds (aka beans) you can dry for later. The protein that dried beans provide makes them a staple part of diets across the world, and they're quicker to crop than runners, making them a highly useful part of any zombie garden.

French beans have two habits. Some twine up poles, others stay low and bushy. Both take up almost the same amount of ground space and come in multiple varieties, producing everything from big, mottled scarlet beans to tiny white ones. Not all are equally good for eating fresh and dry, so to cover all angles, plant several varieties – just remember they all need warmth, and a frost will wipe them out.

Climbing varieties don't get as tall or as heavy as runner beans do, so individual poles or cane wigwams two metres high will be fine for support; tie them in to start with, then let them find their own way upwards. Dwarf beans don't really need support, but pushing bits of twig around them at planting time stops them flopping and keeps birds and cats off.

Each plant will only crop for a few weeks, so to maximize supplies of fresh beans – and minimize the risk of losing a whole crop to bad weather or pests – stagger your plantings by sowing in batches every three weeks or so from April until July.

> A plant's habit is not a description of its drug problem. No – it's gardener-speak for the manner in which something grows.

HOW TO GROW FRENCH BEANS

How many?   Eighteen plants will provide dried beans for one survivor-day of protein + seven days' folate[68]

On the table   Fresh, summer to early autumn; dried, year round

Rotation group   Legumes

Plants per m²   Twenty-four

Sowing   French beans can be tricky to germinate – but we can help. In April, a week before sowing, open your seed packets to allow the contents to absorb some atmospheric moisture. Then sow one or two beans to an 8 cm pot, 5 cm deep. Keep at 16° C – not actually hot, more the sort of temperature you might get on a spring day in the south of France – and in compost no wetter than a wrung-out sponge, otherwise they'll rot. After germination (around fourteen days), thin to one seedling per pot and keep somewhere warm and bright until they're 10 cm high. Plant out once frosts have finished, 10–15 cm apart for dwarf varieties, 20–23 cm apart for climbers.

Feeding   Use an all-purpose fertilizer at planting time.

Watering   Keep moist from when flower buds begin to form until pods begin to yellow.

Harvesting   You can eat green pods almost as soon as you see them, but for maximum nutrition wait until they're about 7.5–10 cm long, then nip them off their stalks. Pick every few days to keep more coming. Once pods start to look bumpy, the beans inside are beginning to develop: leave them on the plant until the pods are brown and wrinkly, then harvest as for runner beans.

Main enemies   **Mice** eat the seed, so germinate indoors. **Slugs** attack when plants are young. **Birds** peck at leaves at planting time; protect youngsters with twigs, fleece or net.

Pot-ability   All kinds of French beans do great in pots 15+ cm deep. For climbers, try 'Borlotto Lingua di Fuoco' for pretty, red-and-white dried beans, or 'Banette' for fresh green pods. Of the dwarf varieties, 'Aquilon' is prolific, and 'Jacob's Cattle' makes excellent beans for drying. Water them all really well, and from June, feed weekly with a liquid high-K fertilizer.

SPROUTING BROCCOLI
Brassica oleracea

Sprouting broccoli is easy to grow and, like its close relative kale, will stand through both summer and the coldest days of winter, giving you a hit of immune-boosting vitamins C and A whenever it pushes out its spears of flower heads.

In the apocalypse, you'll have to ignore all the lovely, quick-growing hybrid varieties and stick to OP purple sprouting broccoli. Which is no bad thing, as although it takes time to get going, it has a long cropping period and comes in two varieties: 'Early Sprouting' for a February to May harvest and 'Late Sprouting' for a harvest split between November and the following spring. To keep the broccoli supplies steady for nine to ten months of the year, use both varieties and sow in batches as per the timings on the right.

And if meanwhile you're wondering where the broccoli-broccoli is – the kind with one big, fat, show-off head – gardeners call this 'calabrese'. Calabrese have very similar demands and pretty much identical nutritional value to the sprouters. And they usually form florets from midsummer onwards, making them a useful way to fill the gap between crops of early and late sprouting broccoli.

HOW TO GROW SPROUTING BROCCOLI

How many?	One plant will provide spears for five survivor-days of vitamin C
On the table	February to May, then October/November
Rotation group	Brassicas
Plants per m²	Four
Sowing	Monthly from March to end of May, sow 'Early Purple' in 5 cm pots, two seeds to a pot, 2 cm deep. Keep a little above 10° C until germination (seven to twelve days). Remove the weakest seedling from each pot and grow the survivor on somewhere bright but cool until 8 cm high (roughly four weeks after sowing). Then harden off and plant out 60 cm apart in every direction. In March, sow a single batch of 'Late Purple', as above; plant out at 60 cm apart in all directions. This sowing will give you an autumn crop. For a very early crop the following spring, sow another batch of 'Late Purple' in June, as above; plant out 45 cm apart in all directions, and give some frost protection (fleece or insect mesh) in autumn.
Feeding	Use an all-purpose fertilizer at planting-out time.
Watering	Keep young plants moist, but tail off watering in mid-August so they don't put on too much late, frost-sensitive growth.
Harvesting	Pick the central flower shoot once it reaches 15 cm long, then pick side shoots, a few at a time, as they appear. Snap or cut off shoots about 10 cm from their heads, while they're still green and tightly closed.
Main enemies	As for kale. Plus **whitefly** might be a problem in very early spring: wipe them off or spray with a mild solution of soapy water.
Pot-ability	'Early Purple' will get way too big and top-heavy, but a June sowing of 'Late Purple' should work, as long as you use really wide containers 45+ cm deep: troughs or dustbins should do it.

STRAWBERRIES
Fragaria x ananassa

You know what a strawberry is, so all we'll say here is that we'd recommend you stick to what are known as perpetual, or everbearing, varieties. These have a first heavy crop in June, then take a little rest before starting up a drip feed of fruit that carries on until early autumn.

Strawberries are undemanding plants and don't need half the fretting over that many garden books suggest. Viz:

- Don't bother planting through a plastic sheet mulch. This makes it very tricky to get the watering right, and weeds will still grow up through the planting holes.
- Don't bother laying straw underneath fruit to keep it clean – because you'll wipe or wash off any splodges of earth before eating, right? And the straw will be a lovely home for slugs and fungal spores.
- Don't bother mucking about with covering plants using cloches or fleece in an effort to get more or earlier fruit. This only encourages mites, mildew and weevils.

In fact we'd say there are just two 'dos': do leave tatty leaves on in winter to protect the crown, or growing point, from frost. And to maximize yields, do cut off runners – baby plants that creep away from their parent plant on long strand-like stems with a knot of small white rootlets at the end. Whenever you see a runner, pinch the long stem off close to the mummy plant and either throw it away or pot it up to stock a new strawberry bed.

Actually, that's a third 'do': plant a new strawberry bed every other year. Because although these are perennial plants that should in theory last for ages, sooner or later most cultivated varieties will succumb to various viruses and their crop production-rate reduces. After plants have cropped for three to four years, dig them out and burn them; the ash can go onto the new bed for a potassium kick. And as long as you remembered to start a new bed, you'll still have plenty of fruit.

HOW TO GROW STRAWBERRIES

How many?   One plant will provide fruit for seven survivor-days of vitamin C

On the table   June to October

Rotation group   None, but don't replant a site with strawberries within three years

Plants per m²   Three

Planting   Ideally, plant out in August/September for a crop the following spring, spacing plants 45 cm apart in rows one metre apart. Water in well. If you have to plant in spring or early summer, nip off flower buds the first year to let the plants establish – they'll crop much better in all the subsequent years.

Feeding   Apply an all-purpose fertilizer in late winter, just before growth starts. Apply a liquid high-K fertilizer in late spring, and again once the first tiny green fruit are starting to show.

Watering   Keep moist when establishing and while fruits are starting to swell.

Harvesting   Pick on dry, warm days, when the fruit is fully red.

Main enemies   **Botrytis** is a fluffy white fungal infection that turns berries brown and mushy-looking while still on the plant. It's best avoided by keeping things airy and not too humid: water first thing in the morning using seep hoses, and don't cover plants with cloches or thick layers of mulch. **Birds and squirrels** love strawberries as much as people do, so cover with netting or chicken wire as soon as the flowers start to show. And then there's **slugs**. Surprise!

Pot-ability   The fact that commercial growers often plant their strawbs in raised rows of growbags should tell you all you need to know. Choose any variety you like, plant in containers 10+ cm deep, and never let them dry out entirely.

BEETROOT
Beta vulgaris subsp. *vulgaris*

Beetroot is a versatile, easy grower, with some varieties good for sowing early to eat in summer and others for midsummer sowings that give autumn crops. Nutritionally, they're all zingers.

Along with broccoli, beetroot is one of the most antioxidant-rich veg that UK survivors can grow without the help of a greenhouse.[69] The leafy, red- or yellow-veined tops of spring-sown beets are a pretty unbeatable source of calcium and iron through the summer months. And stored in boxes or left in the ground under a mulch of straw or bracken, the roots from later, heavier varieties will keep the calories coming through the winter.

Of these, it's the white Altissima varieties, aka sugar beet, that have the highest sweetness and calorific value, though most are so tough they have to be processed into sugar before humans can get the benefit. Despite this, they're worth growing, as making home-brewed beet sugar could be an apocalyptic lifesaver: if you don't believe us, take a look at Chapter 6.

One oddity about beetroot: its little wrinkled 'seeds' are actually packages containing two or three embryonic plants, so you may get several seedlings popping up in each sowing-spot; thin these down to one ASAP so that the survivor grows away well.

Keep sowing direct every twenty days from late April until midsummer, then stop; sow any later than that and temperatures may be too high for good-quality roots to develop.

HOW TO GROW BEETROOT

How many?	Fifteen plants will provide roots and leaves for one day's calories + fifteen days' vitamin C + three days' iron[70]
On the table	May to February
Rotation group	Neutral
Plants per m²	Forty
Sowing	Beet that suffers a prolonged cold snap while it's still small is prone to making flowers, not roots. So for your first batch, sown in early March, use a bolt-resistant variety like 'Boltardy', sowing in 5 cm module trays, one seed to a module, 2.5 cm deep. Keep at 10° C until germination (seven to twenty days), then grow on somewhere bright and cool until they're about 5 cm high. Harden off for at least a week, then plant out 10 cm apart in rows, with 30 cm between rows.

Sow the next batch direct in late April, 3–5 cm apart in trenches of finely raked soil 2.5 cm deep and 30 cm apart. Draw the soil back over and keep moist until germination, then thin out to 10 cm apart. |
Feeding	Use a high-P fertilizer on the site a few weeks before sowing/planting out. Avoid high-N feeds or you'll get loads of leaves but minimal roots.
Watering	Slow and steady is best, so roots don't split because of sudden overwatering or go woody because of underwatering.
Harvesting	In summer, pick a few leaves from each plant when they're around 15 cm high. Roots are ready to eat from golf-ball size up; dig them up as you need them, and cut off the leaf stalks a little way from the top of the root.
Main enemies	**Cutworm** can chomp young roots off below soil level so that rows of leaves suddenly collapse. Keeping rows well weeded seems to help. **Birds** will eat direct-sown seed, so cover with fleece until germination. **Slugs** will attack young module-sown plants.
Pot-ability	'Boltardy' is the easiest to grow, but other mid-size varieties to try in pots at least 25 cm deep include 'Boldor', with a lovely golden root, and red-and-white-striped 'Chioggia'.

SWISS CHARD
Beta vulgaris subsp. *cicla*
var. *flavescens*

Because you're used to Latin now, you'll have spotted that Swiss chard is beetroot with a different surname. Which makes sense, because chard is basically upside-down beetroot.

Chard puts all its energy into its spectacular leaves: wide, crinkled and shiny, with broad white, red or yellow veins, these cook and taste much like spinach. And like spinach, they're positively clanging with iron.

But chard is better than spinach in every way. It doesn't bolt and go bitter the minute the days get too long or too short, or if you don't give it exactly the right amount of water at exactly the moment it wants it. Chard is also a proper cut-and-come-again crop, which means you can cut off a few leaves at a time – and, magically, new ones will keep coming. Even more importantly in an apocalypse, if you sow a batch in late summer and cover the young plants with fleece or a cloche come autumn, they'll keep on growing – slowly, but growing – right through winter and into the following spring.

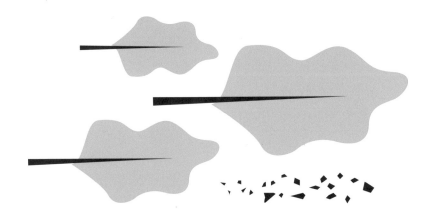

HOW TO GROW SWISS CHARD

How many?	Two plants provide leaves for one survivor-day of iron + five days' vitamin C + two days' magnesium
On the table	June to March
Rotation group	Neutral
Plants per m²	Fourteen
Sowing	Chard is one of the very few zombie-garden veg we'd recommend always sowing direct, as long as the soil temperature is above 5° C – ideally higher than 10° C. For an early crop of leaves, in April rake the soil finely and water gently, then make shallow trenches 2.5 cm deep and 45 cm apart. Sow a seed into these trenches every 3 cm or so, then rake the soil back over. Keep moist until germination (five to seven days), then thin gradually during the next couple of weeks to 20 cm apart. Sow further batches in the same way every month until early August.
Feeding	Add an all-purpose fertilizer just before sowing.
Watering	Should only be necessary during spring and summer dry spells.
Harvesting	Cut a few leaves off plants, 5 cm or so above the soil level, as soon as they are large enough to be worth eating. Harvest regularly to keep new leaves coming.
Main enemies	**Slugs** might bother very young seedlings, but not as much as they would spinach. Are you detecting a theme here?
Pot-ability	Pretty much all varieties of chard will romp away in pots 20+ cm deep, as long as you choose the right size: 'Fordhook Giant' and 'Orange Oriole' need wide containers, while 'Rainbow' and 'Ruby Red' are fine in narrower ones. In all cases, use a liquid high-N fertilizer once plants are 15 cm or so high.

PUMPKINS AND SQUASH
Cucurbita moschata/maxima

Before we go any further, let's get something clear. Squash are pale yellow and either acorn- or bottle-shaped. Pumpkins are round and orange. Winter squash are green, blue or multicoloured and look like either a pouffe or a turban. Botanists reading this will be having a fit, but at least now the rest of us know what we're talking about.

As for families: whether *C. moschata* or *C. maxima*, you needn't worry too much about which family your squash/pumpkin/winter squash comes from; *moschata* varieties tend to cope better with really steamy weather is all. And all of them make big, blundering plants that can be really satisfying to grow.

Sprawling, slightly prickly stems bear lobed leaves as big as your palm,  with wide-mouthed, yellow flowers that swell into heavy fruit. Stored correctly, these are a useful source of vitamin C through the winter. But they need a long, warm summer to fruit properly, so they won't do well in very cold zombie gardens.

Weight for weight, squash offer almost double the calories and vitamin C of pumpkins and winter squash – but as the latter two are thicker skinned, they tend to store for longer. All give you much the same weight of crop per plant, though you should only expect to get one or two big fruits on a pumpkin plant but five to six smaller, neater chaps on a squash.

Varieties come in two habits. Some will grow low and bushy, others wander all over the shop. You can grow the wanderers up tripods or over arches and frames if you want, but it's definitely easier to leave varieties with very big fruit to trail about at ground level.

HOW TO GROW PUMPKINS AND SQUASH

How many?	Four plants provide fruit for seventy-six survivor-days of vitamin C + three days' calories[71]
On the table	September to February
Rotation group	Neutral
Plants per m²	One
Sowing	In April, sow seeds individually in 9 cm pots. Smaller squash seeds should go 1 cm deep, pumpkins up to 3 cm deep. They're prone to rotting, so sow on their edges rather than lying flat, and germinate as fast as you can – they will sprout at 18° C, but a steady 22° C will get things moving much quicker. Cover pots with clear plastic bags or lids until germination (four to fourteen days). Grow on somewhere warm and bright until the third jagged leaf appears, then harden off. Plant out smaller-fruited varieties 90 cm apart in all directions, really big-fruited varieties 1.2 m apart in all directions. If the weather is still a bit less than summery, tuck them under cloche hoops for the first few weeks.
Feeding	The bigger the fruit, the hungrier the plant, so add plenty of all-purpose fertilizer at planting-out time. (If you're using well-rotted manure, fill a hole about a spade's depth and width with it, then plant directly into the manure.) Use a liquid high-K feed every two weeks after planting until fruit has begun swelling.
Watering	To stop fruits from splitting, keep water supplies steady. In dry areas, help irrigate roots by sinking an old flower pot into the soil next to each plant and watering into it.
Harvesting	Pinch off the growing tips of vines after three to seven fruit have started to form – the bigger the variety, the fewer fruit you should leave on each plant. Once skins have hardened enough not to dent when you push a fingernail into them – and at the latest before the first frost – cut off the green stem at least 5 cm from the top of each fruit. Leave in the hottest, sunniest spot you have to finish hardening, then brush off any dirt.
Main enemies	**Mice** will eat seed, so germinate indoors. **Slugs** – shock! – will attack young leaves. After that, the biggest foe is **powdery mildew**. **Cucumber mosaic virus** stunts and curls leaves, mottling them greeny-yellow: pull up and burn any affected plants and don't use their fruit for saving seed.[72]
Pot-ability	Large varieties are generally too hungry for pot-growing, but smaller-fruited squash such as 'Green Kuri', 'Waltham Butternut' or 'Tromboncino' will cope with containers 45 cm deep, particularly if you use a rich compost.

GARLIC
Allium sativum

Garlic has more to offer than charming breath. From the first late-spring harvest of green garlic to the last of the stored bulbs in midwinter, it makes for a steady supply of vitamins C as well as B6 and calcium. Plus it's full of powerful antibacterial, antifungal and immune-supporting compounds. It can't print your photos or sell you nasty throat sweets, but in every other way garlic is basically a post-apocalyptic Boots.

In a zombie garden, you'll grow garlic not from seed but from nursery-bred bulbs broken into individual cloves. Varieties fall into one of two camps, soft-neck and hard-neck. Hard-necks are meant to have marginally the better taste, but soft-necks generally store better, so they win the apocalypse garlic war. To extend the eating season, grow early and late soft-necks. Purple-skinned varieties will have the most vitamin C, while white-skinned varieties have higher levels of antioxidants,[73] so try to grow some of each.

We'd also recommend elephant garlic, *A. ampeloprasum*, particularly if your zombie garden is on heavy soil. It's not strictly the same species as garlic-garlic, and has slightly lower proportions of vitamins and minerals[74] – but it is the only other allium with almost exactly the same antibacterial and antifungal properties.[75] And weight for weight, it's a winner. Elephant garlic is huge: though you plant it at the same rate per square metre as garlic, its bulbs are two to four times as big, so it makes for a higher nutritional yield. Plus its milder, less flame-thrower flavour makes it easier to eat in bulk – and/or breathe onto fellow survivors.

> If you're not in looting distance of specialist garlic nurseries, you might have to grab a fistful of bulbs from the supermarket. But it'll be risky: there's no guarantee they'll be either virus-free or a variety that will cope with the British climate.

HOW TO GROW GARLIC

How many?	Four plants will provide bulbs for four survivor-days of vitamin B6 + three days' vitamin C
On the table	May to January
Rotation group	Roots and alliums
Plants per m²	Twenty-four
Sowing	Nearly all garlic varieties need around six to eight weeks of proper cold weather to develop well. That means getting them in the ground just before the first frosts, usually in October or November.
	Use a dibber to make holes 4 cm deep, 15–18 cm apart, in rows 30 cm apart. If this gets boring, imagine you're Buffy repeatedly driving a stake into a group of vampires. Drop one clove into each hole, pointy end up, then draw the soil back over and water in. Depending on the weather, you should start to see green shoots appear within three to six weeks.
Feeding	Add an all-purpose fertilizer immediately after sowing. Add a high-K fertilizer in mid-spring, when new growth kicks in.
Watering	Keep moist but not waterlogged until germination, and again once growth restarts in spring. To avoid rotting the bulbs, stop watering as soon as the leaves begin to yellow.
Harvesting	Soft-necks are ready for forking out of the ground when leaves are fully yellow and have flopped over – depending on the variety, this can be any time from May to late August. Hard-neck leaves don't flop, so harvest them when the leaves begin to yellow, usually between late May and early August. Lay whole plants out somewhere airy and warm, but not searingly hot. Leave them to cure for ten to fourteen days, or until the skins of the bulbs are papery. Rub off the dirty outer skin and carefully cut off the roots. Kept ventilated and at 10–17° C, they should last four to five months.[76]
	Harvest whole elephant garlic bulbs in May and June, or let them flower and leave them in place until autumn, when they'll have split into individual, storable cloves.
Main enemies	Garlic is generally trouble-free – the most common problem is **birds** pecking up newly sown cloves, so either fleece or net until shoots are 5 cm high.
Pot-ability	Any variety of garlic will do well in well drained pots 15+ cm deep. Keep moist from spring until the leaves start to yellow, then stop watering to allow bulbs to harden.

COURGETTES
Cucurbita pepo

We love a dual-purpose plant, and courgettes are exactly that. In August, green-skinned, vitamin-rich fruit sprouts from their prickly stems quicker than you can say 'let's make ratatouille'.

Any you miss will continue to grow and swell until by autumn – magic! – they've become marrows, with the potential to store for up to six months.

Like their cousins squash, courgettes are warm-weather plants, so don't plant them out until the frosts are just a vague memory. Varieties either grow fairly upright and stiff or long and trailing, but either way nearly all of them will produce fruit that are green or yellow and, well, courgette-shaped. Except the handful that, like 'Jack Be Little', are round and orange. Clearly they identify as pumpkins: seeing as they grow like pumpkins and eat like pumpkins, that's fine by us.

If all you can find is packets of marrow seed, grab them instead – they're just courgettes that have been bred to grow extra big.

HOW TO GROW COURGETTES

How many?	One plant will provide fruit for sixteen survivor-days of vitamin C + three days' thiamine
On the table	August; as marrows, September to January
Rotation group	Neutral
Plants per m²	One
Sowing	As for squash. Plant out at 90 cm apart in all directions – feel free to grow trailing varieties up supports, though any grown for marrows are easiest left on the ground.
Feeding	As for squash.
Watering	As for squash.
Harvesting	Use a knife to cut courgettes away from the main plant stem when they're about 10–15 cm long; you may need to do this every other day in the glut days of August. They won't store, so either eat fresh or make chutney. Marrows should stay on the plant as long as possible to cure but need to be harvested before the first frost. Cut their stems at least 5 cm away from the fruit, brush off any dirt and store somewhere cool, dark and well ventilated, where they should last from two to six months.
Main enemies	All as for squash – though **slugs** really, really love courgette leaves and fruit: use every weapon you have to keep them off.
Pot-ability	Compact varieties of bush courgettes, such as 'Verde di Milano', will crop well in pots 45+ cm deep. Marrows will be harder, but if you use a compost at Bill Gates-level of richness and are maniacal about feeding and watering, it could be worth a try.

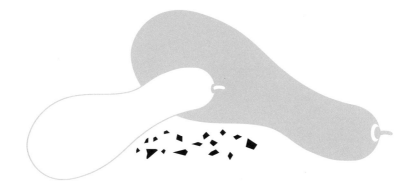

PARSNIPS
Pastinaca sativa

Let's get this over with from the start. Yes, parsnips look a bit like male genitals. But they're also a sweet-tasting, sustaining source of vitamin C right through the darkest days of winter. And there's only really one rule to growing them: sow fresh seed.

Also, don't sow too soon. Or too late. And don't be impatient.

OK, four rules. Why?

First, even at its freshest, parsnip seed seems unwilling to germinate; once more than a year old, it just plain refuses. Second, though in theory germination starts in temperatures as low as 2°C, in practice seed will rot if you sow it in cold, wet soils. But if you delay sowing until soils are really warm and friendly (parsnips sulk if you move them, so this is one of those few zombie-garden plants you pretty much have to sow where they're to grow) the plants won't have time to make proper roots before the frosts start. Also, parsnips are terrible slowcoaches. It's often three weeks or longer after sowing before the green seedlings start to show, which can be dispiriting.

But once up, parsnips are a simple, undemanding plant. As long as you keep them well weeded, they don't need feeding – you shouldn't even bother adding compost unless your soil is a total disaster. Though traditionally a light-soil crop, they'll do fine in all but the most waterlogged clays. And they don't take up storage space indoors, as you can leave roots in place over winter – in fact, they actually taste sweeter after a frost.

Best of all, whenever the apocalypse gets really boring, you can spend an evening deciding which of your crop look most like male genitals.

HOW TO GROW PARSNIPS

How many?	Sixteen plants will provide roots for one survivor-day of calories + twelve days' vitamin C
On the table	October to March
Rotation group	Roots and alliums
Plants per m²	Twenty-six
Sowing	Between March and mid-April, when the soil is between 7–15° C, draw out trenches of finely raked, stone-free soil 2 cm deep, 30 cm apart. Water these gently using a fine rose, then sow one seed every couple of centimetres. Draw dry soil back along the row and, unless you're sowing in very dry conditions, don't water again until germination.
	Parsnip seed typically has a 50–60 per cent germination rate, so only expect to see half your seed come up, but once it does (patience!), gradually thin out to one plant every 15 cm. Hoe out weeds every week or so.
Feeding	Don't bother: too much N will make the plants grow green tops instead of white bottoms.
Watering	Minimal, but steady – letting soil get bone dry will turn roots woody, but a sudden burst of overwatering will make them split.
Harvesting	You can start to harvest baby parsnips as soon as roots are 7 cm long, but for maximum yields wait until the foliage begins to turn yellow and die back, then fork roots out of the ground as you need them. If your soil is very wet or likely to freeze concrete hard in midwinter, lift the whole lot soon after the first frost and store somewhere cool.
Main enemies	**Canker** is a fungal disease that mostly attacks in acid, wet soils, making roots develop rough brown spots and eventually rot. A bit of spotting won't stop them being edible, though, so in an apocalypse it isn't really worth worrying about – just don't grow 'snips on the same site for a few years.
Pot-ability	'Suttons Student', 'Tender and True' and sturdy 'Turga' should all do well in containers 40+ cm deep. Avoid longer-rooted kinds like 'Hollow Crown'.

CARROTS
Daucus carota subsp. *sativus*

Before the apocalypse, carrots were so cheap to buy you'd think they must be easy to grow. In fact, they're tricky both to germinate and to thin, and require a lot of faffing about with insect mesh.

Still, their vitamin load is high, and with good timing you can keep crops coming for three-quarters of the year. So once the zombies hit, we'd say that, like Jennifer Aniston in a L'Oréal ad, they're worth it.

There's a vast number of varieties that come in different shapes, sizes and even colours. These fall into roughly four groups, each of which is suitable for growing at different times of year. This is complicated. So to help you remember which is which when you're grabbing seed, you might find this old poem useful:

> *For carrots in spring, thou must in*
> *autumn rush*
> *And sow Nantes-types under a*
> *cloche.*
> *For roots to eat in midsummer's*
> *days,*
> *In spring sow loads of Chantenays.*
> *For winter crops, take a hoe,*
> *And in midsummer get on and sow*
> *Several packets of Autumn King or*
> *Berlicum-type varieties.*

OK, it's not old, and it's not a poem. You try finding a rhyme for Berlicum.

Whichever season you're sowing in, pick varieties to match your plot. Shallower, dry soils will suit small, quick, round-rooted varieties. Deep, moist soils can take long-rooted, slower-growing kinds. All kinds need to be kept well weeded, and you'll need to be obsessive about preventing carrot fly – the root-munching bloodhound of the insect world – from sniffing them out. This means:

- Using carrot-fly-resistant varieties whenever you can.
- Sowing the bulk of your crop in May, after the first egg-laying season has finished.
- Thinning out in the morning, when the flies are meant to be less active, and by pinching off seedling tops rather than pulling up the scentalicious roots.
- Keeping the whole lot covered throughout the growing season with cloche hoops and insect mesh tucked into the ground.

HOW TO GROW CARROTS

How many?	Five plants will provide roots for one survivor-day of vitamin C + nine days' vitamin A
On the table	Late April to early December
Rotation group	Carrots and parsnips
Plants per m²	Forty
Sowing	Once soil temperatures are 10° C or higher, use a hoe to draw out trenches of moist, finely raked soil 1.5 cm deep and 15 cm apart. Sow a seed every centimetre or so, then rake soil back over down the row. Keep moist until germination (seven to twenty-one days). Seedlings probably won't appear all at once, so wait until at least a month after sowing before thinning to 5 cm apart (short/round varieties) or up to 10 cm (long-rooted varieties). Repeat monthly until the end of July. In well-drained soil, overwintering sowings can go in the ground in early October, covered with fleece or cloche hoops.
Feeding	Don't bother.
Watering	Maintain at moist-ish during spring and summer dry spells; otherwise, leave them be.
Harvesting	You can begin to eat carrots when they're still very small, though for maximum yield leave them in the ground for at least ten weeks, then fork them out as you need them.
Main enemies	**Slugs** eat seedlings and roots particularly in warm, wet autumns. **Carrot fly** you know about. **Wireworm** you also know about: as well as potatoes, it'll snack on carrots.
Pot-ability	If you're surviving on a clay-heavy site, carrots will actually yield better in containers than in open ground. Long-rooted varieties like 'Giant Red' or 'Scarlet Nantes' will need a pot roughly four times their own depth. The short, round kinds (e.g. 'Chantenay Red Core' or 'Oxhella') should crop well in pots 20 cm deep.

Though many carrot-fly-resistant varieties are **F1** cultivars, you can find one or two – like 'Sytan' – that are open-pollinated.

ONIONS
Allium cepa

Onions are another one of those crops that don't have masses of calories. But they do have a surprising amount of vitamin C. And because they store through the winter, that makes them a key player in a zombie garden.

Before the apocalypse, you could save time by buying 'sets': little mini-onions about the size of a clove of garlic, which you planted out between late March and late April. But sets were often prone to bolting, making flowers in their first year instead of bulbs. And as you won't be able to get sets after the first apocalyptic year, you might as well grow onions from seed straight away.

Red, white or shallot, all onions have a few basic needs. Any stress when they're young will make the plants bolt in their first year, so don't let them dry out, don't overwater and don't plant out if the weather is very wet and cold. If they do start to send up flower stalks, snip them off at the base straight away. Onions are also really susceptible to being shaded out by weeds, so hoe weekly until the bulb tops begin to swell above the soil surface. After that, weed by hand, otherwise you will inevitably damage the bulbs, and damaged bulbs don't store.

What size bulbs you get depends on how much space you give seedlings at planting-out time. As giant-vegetable competitions will be a thing of the past, there's no need for men to inflate their flagging self-esteem by growing single bulbs in acres of empty space. If instead they sow and plant out in clumps as described on the right, individual onions will, yes, be smaller, but weight for weight you'll get similar yields – and, vitally, use less of that valuable seed compost.

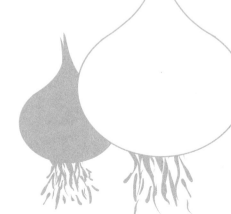

HOW TO GROW ONIONS

How many?	Seven plants will provide bulbs for one survivor-day of vitamin C
On the table	August to February
Rotation group	Roots and alliums
Plants per m²	Forty
Sowing	In late February or early March, in 5 cm module trays, five seeds to a module, 1 cm deep. Keep at 10–20° C until germination (twenty-one days), when you'll see what look like tiny blades of grass. Thin these seedlings to three or four per module, and grow on somewhere cool and bright for a couple of weeks. Then harden off in late March. If the leaves start to yellow at the tips before you're ready to plant out, either pot the module clumps on into 7.5 cm pots or give them a dose of liquid all-purpose fertilizer. In early April, plant out clumps without separating the individual plants, 25 cm apart in all directions.
Feeding	Don't bother.
Watering	Keep it steady at no more than moist-ish until early July, then stop.
Harvesting	Once leaves have yellowed and flopped over, wait for a dry, sunny day, then fork out of the ground – carefully or you'll damage the basal plates (where the roots grow from) and the bulbs won't store well. Arrange them in a single layer somewhere really warm, dry and airy, and leave them until their tops and roots are completely shrivelled and outer skins are papery dry. Store as for garlic.
Main enemies	**Slugs** eat onion leaves throughout the plant's life. **Birds** will peck at new green shoots; cover with fleece until established. **Rust** appears as orange spots on leaves and reduces yields; it often starts on leeks then jumps to onions, so don't grow both in the same season. **Onion downy mildew** coats leaves with grey felt from May on and will eventually rot the bulbs as well; dig them up and eat asap. **Onion white rot** is more serious, though you often won't know you've got it until harvest time, when you'll see a white and fluffy mould clustered round the roots. Bulbs won't store, so burn the lot. And don't try to grow onions in the same soil for – sorry – twenty years.
Pot-ability	Onions don't cope well with high humidity, so crowding them in pots makes them more prone to mildew. Growing varieties of spring or bunching onions such as 'Ischikrona', 'White Lisbon' or 'Early Paris White' will work, though: sow as above, but at a rate of ten seeds to a module. Once they're germinated and hardened off, plant into 20 cm deep pots, without separating the clumps.

TURNIPS
Brassica rapa

Turnips are a multipurpose crop, which makes them perfect for an apocalypse. The roots are big on vitamin C, and spring sowings of early varieties can be ready to harvest within six weeks, while they're still small and tender enough to eat raw.

Later, larger-rooted varieties need cooking but can store for several months into winter. Meanwhile, late-summer sowings planted out close together will provide a leafy crop of spring greens, a first-rate source of folate and vitamins A and C in the hungry month of May. About their only disadvantage is that all varieties need to be kept well weeded, as turnips are not great at shading out their own competition.

They are, however, another of the handful of zombie-garden veg we'd recommend sowing direct: they're cool-season crops and fairly pest resistant, so you don't gain much by starting them under cover. Because turnips are so quick to crop, you can sow them between rows of other, slower-maturing plants to get maximum use of your soil space.

Just be aware that, though it's a root crop, turnip is biologically a brassica, so don't put it in space recently vacated by its cousins broccoli, calabrese or (if you choose to grow it) swede.

HOW TO GROW TURNIPS

How many?   Four plants will provide beans for one survivor-day of protein[77]

On the table Fresh, late spring to late summer; dried, year round

Rotation group Brassicas

Plants per m² Earlies, twenty-nine; maincrop, eighteen; spring greens, 133

Sowing For early varieties, once the soil reaches 7–10° C (usually sometime between late January and late March), sow one seed every couple of centimetres, 2 cm deep, in rows 30 cm apart. Cover with fleece until germination (seven to ten days, longer if the weather is very cold), then thin to 15 cm apart.

For larger maincrop varieties, sow every six weeks from April to early August, thinning to 23 cm apart. For a spring harvest of leaves, sow early varieties in rows 7.5 cm apart in late August to early September, thinning to 10 cm apart in late September and covering with fleece.

Feeding If soil pH is below 6.8, raise it by adding lime or wood ash four weeks before sowing.

Watering Keep moist-ish during late spring and summer.

Harvesting Spring greens are best cut when they're 10–15 cm tall and still tender. Leave around two to three centimetres of stem behind, and with luck and a bit of watering, the plants will give you a second cut of leaves in a few weeks' time.

You can start to lever out turnips grown for roots once they're golf-ball size or bigger, lifting the last of the roots by December.

Main enemies **Flea beetle** will pepper leaves with tiny holes, particularly in dry spells; keep soil moist, water from overhead and/or cover plants with insect mesh. Hungry **pigeons** can attack turnip tops in winter; cover with fleece.

Pot-ability Try 'Golden Ball' or 'Purple Top Milan' for early, medium-sized roots or 'Seven Top' for greens in pots 20+ cm deep – but leave the big-rooted maincroppers for open ground.

CABBAGE
Brassica oleracea

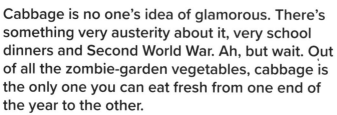

Cabbage is no one's idea of glamorous. There's something very austerity about it, very school dinners and Second World War. Ah, but wait. Out of all the zombie-garden vegetables, cabbage is the only one you can eat fresh from one end of the year to the other.

Steamed or raw, rather than boiled to mush, it's one of the richest sources of vitamin C in the garden, with iron, folate and vitamin A coming along for the ride. And if you ferment it, it makes kimchi. Suddenly, cabbage elevates into the realm of cool.

Varieties divide by growing habit – smooth-leaved white, red or green ballheads, or crinkly-leaved savoys – and cropping period: there is literally a cabbage for all seasons. Red cabbages have the most vitamin C and attract less attention from aphids; savoys have the most iron and survive winter the best; green and white ballheads have the most folate and make the best slaws. Grow them all, following the sowing guide on the right to avoid gluts.

All kinds need plenty of irrigating if the hearts aren't to split – old-time gardeners used to plant cabbage into holes filled with water, in a technique known as puddling in. But slow, regular watering throughout the season is just as effective. Cabbages also tend to rock in high winds, so plant them with their first true leaves sitting at soil level, and mound earth around them as they grow. Eventually their leaves will shade out competition, but keep them well weeded while they're small.

Most of all, remember they're brassicas: you'll have to use the full gamut of anti-slug-pigeon-caterpillar-butterfly weapons, including brassica collars at planting, insect mesh through the summer, and netting over winter.

HOW TO GROW CABBAGE

How many?	Two plants will provide leaves for one survivor-day of iron + five days' folate + eighteen days' vitamin C[78]
On the table	All year
Rotation group	Brassicas
Plants per m²	Four
Sowing	For summer cabbage, sow in early February, in 5 cm pots, one seed per pot, 2 cm deep and keep at 7° C or higher until germination (seven to fourteen days). Harden off once they're around 15 cm high, and in mid-March plant out 40 cm apart in all directions. Winter ballhead cabbage gets sown the same way, in early May, and planted mid-June, 45 cm apart in all directions. Sow and plant out winter savoy cabbages the same way, but start in early June.
Feeding	If soil pH is below 6.8, add lime or wood ash four weeks before planting. Apply an all-purpose fertilizer when planting out spring cabbages and once or twice more in the growing season for summer and autumn cabbages.
Watering	Keep steadily moist through spring, summer and early autumn.
Harvesting	As soon as plants have formed tight, round, leafy heads, cut them away at the base with a sharp knife and chuck the outer leaves. Cut a deep cross into the stalks of spring-, summer- and autumn-harvested cabbages and leave in place for a few weeks to try for a second flush of loose leaves. Cabbage is best eaten fresh, but in winter you can store whole heads in nets somewhere cool and dry for a few weeks.
Main enemies	All as for kale. Plus **flea beetle**. And **gall midge**, but you'll already be using insect mesh to keep off the butterflies, right? And then there's disgusting, waxy-looking **mealy cabbage aphid**, which gathers beneath leaves and on shoot tips. Massacre them by squishing, or spray to death with a dilute solution of soap and water.
Pot-ability	Cabbages are such big plants that only the smallest ballhead varieties would work in pots – and unfortunately we've yet to find any in the UK that aren't F1 cultivars like 'Minicole' or 'Pixie'. Without open ground to grow in, coleslaw will be just a memory. Or maybe that's a good thing?

Sow spring cabbage in late August – but as they won't germinate well above 25°C, at this time of year keep them somewhere semi-shaded until germination. Plant out in early October, 10 cm apart in all directions, then thin gradually to 20 cm.

TOMATOES
Lycopersicon esculentum

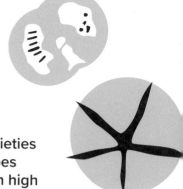

Unless you're very canny about which varieties you grow, the cropping season for tomatoes can be short – perhaps just eight weeks in high summer. But during those few weeks, they are the glory of the zombie garden.

You don't *have* to have a greenhouse or a polytunnel either, as it's a common misconception that toms need really hot conditions. As long as you choose varieties that are billed for outdoor growing, they should do well – though consider sticking to earlier-cropping varieties to avoid blight attacks.

Varieties divide into three groups, each of which need slightly different treatment. To get the best from indeterminate (aka vine) tomatoes, you need to limit their growth to just one central stem. This means obsessively nipping out side shoots from the joints between the main stem and its leaves. Vine toms get very heavy, so need a lot of support. A single bamboo cane won't cut it; either tie vines to stout wooden stakes, or build a strong frame strung with twine to grow the vines up. Outdoor vines will probably only have four or five sets of

ripe fruit before the frosts start, so once the fifth set of fruit has started to swell, nip off the tip of the main stem two sets of leaves above the final truss.

Determinate, or bush, varieties of tomato tend to crop earlier in the season, bear their flowers at the end of every trailing stem, and need less fuss over side shoots and training. It's still good practice to pinch out any side shoots that appear beneath the first truss of flowers, to make sure the main stem grows sturdily enough to stop the plant flopping.

Intermediate, aka semi-determinate, varieties are – and we know this will shock you – a bit vine, a bit bush. For these, you pinch out all the side shoots below the first truss of flowers, and then allow no more than three or five other side shoots to develop per plant, all as low down on the main stem as possible.

HOW TO GROW TOMATOES

How many?	One plant will provide fruit for thirteen survivor-days of vitamin C
On the table	June to early October
Rotation group	Solanums
Plants per m²	Two
Sowing	Sow in early March, in 7 cm pots, two per pot, 1 cm deep. Keep moist at 15–25° C until germination (seven to fourteen days), then thin to one seedling per pot. Grow on somewhere bright and warmish – a closed cold frame, growhouse or windowsill should be fine, though turn pots daily if you're growing on a sill. In early April, prick out into 12 cm pots, putting the root balls at the base of the new pots and burying the seedlings in compost up to their first true leaves. In early May, or when the first flower bud appears, harden off for ten to fourteen days. Plant out when all risk of frost has passed, 40 cm apart for vines, 30–90 cm apart for bushes, and in either case in rows 90 cm apart.
Feeding	Use an all-purpose fertilizer at planting time. Once the first flowers appear, feed weekly with a liquid high-K fertilizer.
Watering	Keep steadily moist-ish from germination to harvest. If tomatoes do dry out once fruit has set, start to rewater gradually or fruit may split.
Harvesting	Pick fruit as they turn red; any that are still green as the first frosts threaten can be used for chutneys.
Main enemies	**Late tomato blight** is the one to fear. Leaves go first translucent, then brown and wilty, and unless you pick them off fast, the rest of the plant will die. Keep foliage as dry and well aired as possible, don't water from overhead and pray like hell to the tomato gods. **Blossom end rot** makes fruit go black at one end. It's caused by erratic and/or excessive watering, so don't do either of those things. **Magnesium deficiency** makes leaves go yellow in the centres, leaving solid bands of green around the veins, and shows up at the bottom of the plant first. It usually means you've been overwatering, giving too much K feed or both; so stop.
Pot-ability	There are tons of OP outdoor varieties to choose from: grow the ever-popular 'Gardener's Delight' if you must, but we'd encourage you to experiment, as outdoor toms can actually be more successful in containers than in open ground. Forget about shallow growbags: use troughs or pots 35+ cm deep, and train stems up trellises or bamboo wigwams. Feed weekly with a high-K fertilizer once flowers appear, and be prepared to water every day in hot weather.

Tomatoes under cover are much less likely to get blight – so if you love toms and have the room, it is worth building a greenhouse or poly to grow them in.

PEAS
Pisum sativum

Of all the veg in a zombie garden, peas can be the trickiest. Not that they're to blame: they actively enjoy the cool and damp of a traditional British summer and don't need high temperatures to germinate or masses of manure to crop.

The problem is this: they taste too good. Mice, slugs, pigeons, weevils, moth grubs – everthing wants to eat them. So by all means grow peas – never mind how sweet they are, the vitamin C they provide in spring should be reason enough – but be ready to jump through a whole load of hoops.

Peas come in three kinds. Mangetout provide young, flat pods; sugar snaps make eat-them-whole swollen pods; podding types are for fresh or dried peas. And the lower-growing the variety, the earlier it crops. So an 'early' pea plant that only grows to 50 cm high will be ready for harvesting two to three months after sowing, while a vigorous maincropper two metres high will be ready after three to four months. If you've only got room for one variety, stick to the big boys: they'll give you a higher yield for the same amount of space.

All need support of some kind. Short, early varieties will be fine scrambling up tall, twiggy branches. Maincrops need much stronger supports, fitted out with something for their tendrils to cling to: an A-frame, wigwam or row of poles, either strung horizontally with lines of twine or with chicken wire fixed across them, will do the job.

Next comes protection. Unless you're surviving in a sterile, wildlife-free zone, you're probably going to need to use a combination of insect mesh and bird netting to keep peas' enemies at bay. But that means almost daily net-removing-and-replacing so that you can perform the following duties:

- killing slugs
- replacing/refilling mousetraps
- watering in hot, dry weather
- getting rid of weeds (which peas seem particularly prone to)
- harvesting to keep the crop coming

See what we mean about hoops?

HOW TO GROW PEAS

How many?	Three plants provide peas for one survivor-day of vitamin C
On the table	June to September
Rotation group	Legumes
Plants per m²	Forty
Sowing	Sow in batches monthly from mid-February to late April, in 5 cm module trays, two to a module, 2.5 cm deep. Keep the seed compost more than just moist (pea seed needs water to swell) and at 10° C or higher until germination (seven to ten days). Then thin to one seedling per cell. Prick out into 9 cm pots and grow on somewhere cool and bright until they're 15 cm high and (relatively) pest-proof. Harden off for a week or so, then plant out 10 cm apart in a double row 25 cm apart.
Feeding	Use an all-purpose fertilizer at planting-out time.
Watering	Not too much between germination and when the shoots reach 50 cm tall, but keep them steadily moist once they're flowering, and also when the pods are swelling.
Harvesting	Once the first pods begin to set, check every few days for readiness: mangetout and sugar snap pods can be picked once they reach 7.5 cm; podding peas should be picked when the pods are swollen but still green and the seed inside has filled out nicely. Pick every few days, starting at the bottom of the plant and working upwards.
Main enemies	**Mice** will raid module trays, so keep them with you in the house, or hang them up high somewhere rodents can't climb/leap/gyrocopter up to. Protect from **birds** with a fence of twigs and/or bird netting. **Slugs** are a problem until plants are 12 cm high or so. **Powdery mildew** can hit leaves in high and late summer, so don't let the soil dry out. **Pea weevil** and **pea moth** are more prevalent from midsummer on, so after May protect rows with insect mesh. **Fusarium root** and/or **neck rots** are more likely to attack and kill individual plants if you overwater. Don't overwater.
Pot-ability	The most vigorous podding varieties, such as 'Ambassador' or 'Alderman', will be too top-heavy for most containers. Instead use 'Hurst Greenshaft' or 'Douce Provence', or very short, very early varieties like 'Havel' and 'Charmette' in pots 20+ cm deep. For sugar snaps, 'Cascadia' is a good container option, and the mangetout 'Norli' grows to only a dinky 50 cm. Remember to give them all some support, and protect as you would in open ground.

THE ZOMBIE GARDEN YEAR

The apocalypse could start at any time. So here's a useful calendar to help you work out what to do and when, whether zombies attack in January or June.

JANUARY – MARCH

	SOW UNDER COVER	SOW DIRECT	PLANT OUT	HARVEST
JAN	Broad beans	Early turnips		Parsnips Swiss chard Kale Savoy cabbage Winter ballhead cabbage Beetroot
FEB	Summer cabbage Beetroot Broad beans Onions Peas	Early turnips	Broad beans[a]	Parsnips Swiss chard Kale Savoy cabbage Winter ballhead cabbage Early purple broccoli Beetroot
MAR	Tomatoes Onions Beetroot Broad beans Early purple broccoli Late purple broccoli Peas	Early turnips Parsnips	Potatoes (all) Broad beans Summer cabbage	Parsnips Swiss chard Kale Savoy cabbage Early purple broccoli Late purple broccoli Turnip tops Early turnips

APRIL – JUNE

	SOW UNDER COVER	SOW DIRECT	PLANT OUT	HARVEST
APR	Autumn cabbage Calabrese Runner beans Early purple broccoli Amaranth French beans Pumpkins & squash Peas Courgettes	Parsnips Beetroot Swiss chard Summer carrots Maincrop turnips	Potatoes (all) Peas Broad beans Onions	Swiss chard Kale Spring cabbage Parsnips Early purple broccoli Late purple broccoli Turnip tops Early turnips
MAY	Winter ballhead cabbage Amaranth French beans Early purple broccoli	Beetroot Swiss chard Summer carrots Maincrop turnips	Beetroot Peas Early purple broccoli Autumn cabbage Late purple broccoli Tomatoes Runner beans Pumpkins & squash Courgettes	Early purple broccoli Beetroot & leaf beet Broad beans[b] Green garlic Spring carrots Early turnips Early peas
JUN	Savoy cabbage Late purple broccoli	Summer carrots Beetroot Swiss chard Autumn carrots Maincrop turnips	Peas Pumpkins & squash Courgettes Amaranth French beans Kale Winter ballhead cabbage Early purple broccoli Calabrese	Garlic Broad beans[b] Strawberries Beetroot & leaf beet Peas Swiss chard Summer cabbage Summer carrots Maincrop turnips First early potatoes

(a) Use fleece or cloches to protect from frost (b) Fresh beans (c) Dried beans

JULY – SEPTEMBER

	SOW UNDER COVER	SOW DIRECT	PLANT OUT	HARVEST
JUL	Runner beans	Swiss chard Autumn carrots Maincrop turnips	French beans Savoy cabbage Kale Early purple broccoli	Peas Summer carrots Garlic Summer cabbage Broad beans[b] French beans[b] Runner beans[b] Calabrese Beetroot Swiss chard Maincrop turnips
AUG	Spring cabbage	Maincrop turnips Swiss chard Turnip tops	Runner beans Kale Late purple broccoli[a] Strawberries	Peas Summer carrots Summer cabbage Courgettes Garlic Second early potatoes Onions Runner beans[b] French beans[b] Broad beans[c] Calabrese Strawberries Beetroot Swiss chard Maincrop turnips
SEP		Turnip tops[a] Over-wintering green manure	Strawberries	French beans[b][c] Runner beans[b][c] Kale Broad beans[c] Calabrese Strawberries Maincrop potatoes Beetroot Swiss chard Pumpkins & squash Autumn carrots Autumn cabbage Marrows Maincrop turnips Amaranth

OCTOBER – DECEMBER

SOW UNDER COVER	SOW DIRECT	PLANT OUT	HARVEST
	Spring carrots[a] Broad beans[a]	Garlic cloves Spring cabbage	Strawberries French beans[c] Runner beans[c] Autumn carrots Autumn cabbage Pumpkin & squash Marrows Swiss chard Kale Calabrese Beetroot Maincrop turnips
			Late purple broccoli Beetroot Maincrop turnips Autumn cabbage Autumn carrots Swiss chard Kale
			Beetroot Autumn carrots Maincrop turnips Parsnips Swiss chard Kale Savoy cabbage Winter ballhead cabbage

OCT

NOV

DEC

(a) Use fleece or cloches to protect from frost (b) Fresh beans (c) Dried beans

MEDIEVAL ON YOUR ASS, LITERALLY

ANIMALS FOR THE APOCALYPSE

What animal bums can do for your zombie garden

The bottom line

Vegans, look away now. This page is for survivors who want to benefit from the nutrients animals can provide – particularly vitamin B_{12}, which plants, frankly, are useless at. It's also for anyone who remembers all the uses of animal manure (and, even though they'd rather forget them, the poo jokes) from Chapter 4.

Why? Because as the old, old tradition of mixed farming showed, keeping animals – who churn out nutrient-rich manure as well as milk and eggs – benefits any zombie gardener who has the space for them. As long as you don't put too many animals on one site, they're past masters at maintaining fertility and on poor ground can actually increase it. Also, they're nice to have around.

Go figure

To decide which animal will best suit your site, think about three things.

First is space. There'll be no processed feed in an apocalypse, so you'll need enough pasture – fields, lawns, the rec at the end of the road – to provide grass in summer and hay all winter. Next, how much nutrition will their milk or eggs provide? (We're ignoring meat, as the apocalypse will have seen enough meaningless death already.) Then consider how much NPK is in their manure. For grass-fed animals, you'll have to do your calcs based on, um, solids alone, as they'll be doing at least half of their weeing in the fields.

To help, here's a handy table, showing you how much nutrient return you'll get from a single square metre of pasture. Simply work out how many square metres of grazing space (or, for chickens, eating-insects space) you've got, multiply that by the figures here and hey presto – you've got some more figures. Plus, we hope, more idea of just how useful animals can be.

HANDY TABLE NO. 14

THE SQUARE-METRE ANIMAL SHOWDOWN

	COW	SHEEP	GOAT	CHICKEN[a]	SHIRE HORSE[b]
FOOD PER DAY[80]	0.7 litres milk[c]	0.3 litres milk[d]	0.4 litres milk[e]	0.7 eggs[f]	260g wheat[g]
CALORIES PER DAY	430 kcals	334 kcals	284 kcals	38 kcals	850 kcals
B$_{12}$ PER DAY	3.14 mcg	2.2 mcg	0.28 mcg	0.28 mcg	0 mcg
PROTEIN PER DAY	23 g	18.5 g	17 g	3 g	25g
FAT PER DAY	23 g	21 g	15 g	4 g	4 g
N PER YEAR[81]	2.3 g	1.6 g	3.3 g	2.3 g	2.8 g
P PER YEAR	1.1 g	0.7 g	1.8 g	1 g	1.5 g
K PER YEAR	1.1 g	1.5 g	3.6 g	0.5 g	2.79 g

Outputs given are all per square metre[79]

Cows

A dairy cow can produce milk for around 305 days a year – as long as you've got a bull to get her pregnant. This means a) you need at least 2.5 acres of reasonable-quality grazing to feed the pair of them and b) you can't be scared of bulls. But per square metre of pasture, a cow will provide you with more vitamin B_{12} than any other animal.

Sheep

A dairy-breed ewe can provide milk for up 180 days a year. Yes, you'll need space for a ram as well – at least a third of an acre for the pair – but rams are much easier to handle than bulls. Plus sheep's milk has the most fat per litre, meaning you can make more cheese from it – and cheese is the best way to store milk nutrients when fridges are just a distant memory.

Chickens

A young hen will produce an average of 260 eggs a year for three years, after which she slows right down – but adding a rooster to the mix means you can rear new hens as you need them. Left to range freely during the day, without any other food from you, the two of them would need around 200 square metres of pasture. But if you're able to feed them home-grown grains, you can keep them in a much smaller space – as little as one square metre each, which makes hens winners in urban zombie gardens.

Goats

It might have less vitamin B_{12} than cow's milk, but goat's milk makes more cheese per litre. Goat manure is dry and easy to collect, plus it gives the most plant nutrients per square metre of pasture. And though a goat and a billy will need slightly more space (just under half an acre) than a ewe and a ram, they're tougher than sheep – animals who, farmers like to say, have a habit of waking up dead.

Horses

A 1,000 kg shire horse won't provide any vitamin B_{12} – unless you eat it. But that would be a waste: in return for just one and a quarter acres of grazing, one shire can plough, harrow, seed and reap up to eight hectares a year, allowing you to grow calorie- and protein-rich cereals on a (pre)-industrial scale. Plus, per square metre, its poo is only beaten on the plant-food front by goats – who, last time we checked, don't do ploughing.

So what all that adds up to is this: you want cows for vitamins, sheep for cheese, goats for manure, hens for eggs and a horse for wheat. For which you'd need the equivalent of 4.63 acres. Remember 'a man with five acres is a rich man indeed'? Indeed.

DUSTBIN DINNERS

No-garden gardeners, alert! You'll have noticed that to grow some of the veg in the previous chapter, you need pretty deep containers. Large terracotta pots could be a real drain on your budget. Luckily, there's no need to cancel your Netflix subscription just so you can do gardening. Instead, think dustbins.

As long as you drill some drainage holes in the bottom, dustbins make excellent containers for greedy, tall or deep-rooted plants. Because they hold plenty of soil, they'll also give you the chance to experiment with large perennial veg plants – the kind you crop from year after year. And if you plan carefully, you can use dustbins to grow the makings of an entire dinner menu, from starter right through to pudding.

Here's how.

1 START WITH THE STARTER

Your dustbin menu begins with globe artichokes, a total deli delicacy. They're slightly alien-looking perennials, with jagged silver leaves that fountain out of the soil in spring, followed in late summer by thick stalks topped with an edible flower that's half thistle, half bed knob. They're big: a metre high isn't unusual, and in open ground they need to be planted about one metre apart. But a single plant will fit well in a dustbin, giving you a crop of several flowerheads a year.

Artichokes mustn't get too hot or too cold. Their seed needs a bit of warmth to germinate, but young plants need several weeks of cool spring nights (at or below 10° C[82]) if they're to flower in their first year. As frosts will kill youngsters, in the UK that pretty much means planting out in early May.

To have your young plants ready at the right time, sow seed in March, in 9 cm pots, 2 cm deep, three seeds to a pot. Keep moist at 16–21° C and in good light until germination (fourteen to twenty-one days), then thin to one seedling per pot. Once young plants are 20 cm or so high, harden off for a week or two. Or just buy young plug plants from a garden centre in mid to late April. Plant these into 9 cm pots and wait until they have five sets of true leaves before moving on to the next step.

2 FILL THE FIRST BIN

Artichokes are greedy but like plenty of drainage, so either fill your dustbin almost to the top with bagged all-purpose compost mixed 3:1 with grit, or mix garden compost, topsoil and sand 2:2:1. (A full dustbin is a heavy dustbin, so get yours in position first: ideally somewhere out of the wind that gets at least six hours of sun a day.) Plant one artichoke per dustbin, water in well and use an all-purpose fertilizer to get growth started. Water well until midsummer – after that, tail off a little.

Once the plant throws up a flower stalk, keep a close eye: don't harvest the bud at the tip until it's at least golf-ball size – though some varieties get much bigger. Cut buds close to the stem using secateurs, and with luck you may get some smaller side-shoot buds forming.

When the top growth has died back for winter, stop watering and wrap the bin in fleece or bubble wrap to protect from frosts. As long as you top up the potting mix with fresh compost and/or manure each year, your artichoke should keep cropping well for several years.

3 SPUDS FOR SECONDS

For the main course, we'd suggest baked potatoes. Not quite as chi-chi as artichoke hearts, but you are prepping for the end of the world, remember? Also, potatoes dug straight from the soil taste completely delicious – even out of a dustbin.

Container-held soil will warm more quickly than open ground, so you can begin planting first-early potato varieties in late February; maincrops can go in up until the end of March. Make a layer 20–25 cm deep at the bottom of a dustbin with either an all-purpose bagged compost or a mix of equal parts garden compost and topsoil. Place three tubers on the surface, keeping them away from the very edge of the bin, and cover with 10 cm compost. Containers heat up easily, so you have to pay some attention to positioning them – if the soil gets too warm, yields will drop. Choose a spot for your bin that gets plenty of light but won't overheat in high summer. Then water well, and cover with fleece if a frost seems likely.

If plain potatoes don't appeal, plant a dustbin with cauliflower – another big, space-hungry plant – and make aloo gobi instead.

4 EARTH UP AND EAT UP

Every time green leaves start to poke their heads above the soil, cover them with a little compost. Once this added layer has reached 20 cm deep, stop and let the tops grow away. Feed every fortnight or so with a liquid all-purpose fertilizer, and don't ever let the· bins dry out completely. First earlies will be ready to harvest about ten weeks after planting, maincrop varieties after twenty weeks. As earlies will have vacated the premises by May or early June, you could refresh the compost and sow a second crop in late July/early August, which should be ready for harvesting before the first frosts.

5 JUST DESSERTS

Your pudding is another delicacy: the sweet, delicate stems of forced rhubarb. Like globe artichoke, rhubarb is a perennial and needs a lot of space: its broad, slightly cupped leaves stand proud on carmine-red stems and can cover at least a metre. That and its greedy nature make it a good fit for dustbins – especially if you use the lids to double up as forcing jars.

You can grow rhubarb from seed in spring, but you won't be able to take a crop until summer the following year, so we'd say buy a plant instead, either bare-rooted rhubarb 'crowns' or in a pot.

In late summer or early autumn, pick a spot that is lightly shaded: those big leaves mean rhubarb needs a lot of moisture and will go to pieces in high heat. Fill your dustbin two-thirds to the top with all-purpose compost mixed 1:1 with bagged farmyard manure, or your own mix of compost, manure and topsoil 1:2:1, then plant the rhubarb so its growing tip sticks slightly proud of the compost surface. Water in well, and wait.

6 FORCE YOURSELF

The first spring after planting, use an all-purpose fertilizer as growth begins. Then put the dustbin lid on, nice and tight – you want to keep UV light out and warmth in. Check weekly to make sure the compost is good and moist. After about six weeks, the plant will have made several long, pale stems topped with wrinkly yellow leaves. Twist these off at the base, discard the (poisonous) leaves, and cook the stalks.

As soon as you've harvested, take the lid off the dustbin, feed the plant again, and don't harvest any further stalks this year. The following year, leave the crown to develop naturally, cutting up to a third of the stalks that grow before the end of June. Top up the manure annually and your plant should go on producing well for around five years. Bon apocalyptic appetit! ✳

A forcing jar can be anything that excludes light from a plant, making it grow extra soft and tender. Gardeners with too much money use special, dome-shaped terracotta pots, but a bucket will work just as well.

6

SELF-PRESERVATION

You will face many difficulties growing food in an apocalypse. But perhaps the trickiest thing to get used to is having either too much of a crop or nothing at all. This week, twenty courgettes. Next week, no courgettes. (Nourgettes?)

Gluts, times when plants produce more than you can eat, are inevitable in a zombie garden. But they can be useful – as long as you can store the excess. Sadly, with the grid down, your fridge-freezer will be no help. Instead you'll have to rely on other, mostly very old ways of extending the shelf life of fruit and veg. And that's what we'll be looking at in this chapter – how to preserve food the non-electric way.

Drying your harvests of fruit and veg, keeping them cool in cellars underground, pickling them in vinegar, and using them to make jams and chutneys are all perfectly possible in an apocalypse, as long as you have a few basic supplies – remember the Looting Lists from Chapter 1? You could also try salting, lactic fermentation (which basically means kimchi) or bottling.

So there are plenty of methods to choose from. But before we get on to how to do all this preserving, there is one other thing we should mention.

It could kill you.

> Sadly, with the grid down, your fridge-freezer will be no help. You'll have to rely on other ways of extending the shelf-life of fruit and veg

IN A PICKLE

Preserving food is potentially as risky as shark-diving with a pork chop in your pants. Yes, traditional methods can all keep food edible for the long term. But get these processes wrong, and you're going down. And it's all the fault of something called *Clostridium botulinum*.

The C-bot, as we like to think of it, is a bacterium which, given the right conditions, thrives in airtight, room-temperature containers of food. While it's thriving, it produces botulin, aka Botox. If instead of injecting this into your face, you accidentally eat some, this is what is likely to happen:

- At some point between six hours and ten days later, your mouth will go dry
- Then your vision will blur
- Then your face muscles will go droopy and you'll start to have trouble swallowing or speaking
- Then your lungs will seize up and you will die
- But probably not before you've had a bad attack of constipation

As a C-bot infection doesn't affect the look or smell of food, this means that probably the most effective way to kill off the evil leader of a rival group is to offer him a jar of your own badly bottled green beans.

It also means you need to think hard about what *are* the safe ways to preserve. So let's look at the options available.

Badly bottled or not, the beans would have been fine if you'd been able to keep them in a fridge: C. botulinum can't operate at temperatures below 3° C.

High-temperature pasteurizing

Heating fruit and vegetables in special self-sealing jars to 121° C kills all bacteria, up to and including mega-tough C-bot spores.

BUT you can only do it with a stove-top pressure canner, a bit of American homesteading kit that you'd be pushed to find in the UK before the apocalypse, never mind after.

Verdict A thousand per cent double-double safe. Though pretty much impossible.

Lactic acid fermentation

If you mix salt with chopped veg – either dry or by submerging them in brine – and then keep them at room temperature, lactobacilli will turn the vegetable sugars into lactic acid. And most bad bacteria can't survive in an acid environment.

BUT while our ancestors happily stored kimchi and sauerkraut in cool cellars for several months, modern food-safety experts insist the only way to be 100 per cent sure of no C-bot is to keep fermented foods in a fridge.

Verdict Possibly iffy, definitely whiffy.

Vinegar pickling

Steeping veg in a solution of vinegar and (usually) some salt works much like lacto-fermentation, except with acetic acid preventing the bacterial activity.

BUT to be sure of being botulin-free without a fridge, you'll have to follow tried-and-tested recipes and – to drive the pickling acids deep into the vegetable tissues – pressure-can the results. As well as only using vinegar with a concentration of 5 per cent acetic acid. Have you used a titration kit recently?

Verdict Only for chemistry graduates.

Cellaring

Because soil temperatures both lag several degrees behind air temperatures and fluctuate less, underground spaces like cellars – or their smaller relatives, clamps – can keep food cool enough to slow down destructive bacterial activity.

BUT in this country cellars and clamps will rarely be cold enough to stop the C-bot, so they're only useful for winter storage of things like fresh potatoes, onions and carrots.

Verdict Safe, if limited. Also, cellars have zombies in them. Always.

> Clamps are lidded pits dug in the ground, often lined with straw, sand or bricks, used to store fresh vegetables through the winter. You could make your own by burying a series of metal dustbins. Though you might prefer to bang your head against a brick wall instead.

Drying

Dehydrating at low heats and with lots of air movement drives out moisture and raises sugar concentrations, both of which extend food's shelf-life. Pre-apocalypse, electric dehydrators were an easy way to get garden produce dry enough to store for up to a year in sealed containers.

BUT post-apocalypse, lengthy, resource-hungry drying in an oven at 60° C/140° F will be the only option, and the results aren't likely to store as well.

Verdict Long-winded.

Jams and chutneys

Sugar is a fabulously effective preservative. Any bacteria that end up in a high-sugar environment will, thanks to the magic of osmosis, quickly shrivel up and die as all the water in their cell structure says 'So long, sucker' and seeps off over to the sweet side of the fence. A jam made by boiling equal amounts of fruit and sugar should, if stored in a sealed, sterilized jar, last pretty much for ever. Mix sugar with equal amounts of vinegar and you can also use it to preserve low-acid vegetables, like green tomatoes, beetroot, corn and courgettes, in the form of chutneys.

BUT... there isn't really a 'but'. After cellaring and pressure-canning, jam- and chutney-making are the safest ways

to preserve without a fridge. That's because the initial boiling kills living bacteria, while the killer combination of acid and sugar stops C. botulinum spores from activating once they've cooled. To be 1,000 per cent spore-free, you should then follow the American practice of boiling your filled jam jars in deep pans of water. But since there have only been sixty-two cases of food botulism recorded in the UK since 1922[83] and none of those cases involved jams or chutneys, if you don't bother, we'd understand.

Verdict Not just for Radio 4 listeners.

If you're not sure how to make jam, take a look at the next Prep for the Pre-Apocalypse (see page 204). And if you're wondering where all the vinegar and sugar you'll need is going to come from, read on.

SUPPLIES AND DEMANDS

We know that supplies of looted sugar and vinegar will eventually disappear. Luckily, there are a few things you can do to eke them out. Both of which, naturally enough, involve gardening.

Beet it

You might assume that all the sugar we eat in this country is made from sugar cane and imported. In fact, up to 50 per cent is homegrown, in the form of sugar beet.[84] This is nothing more than a particularly large, white and sweet variety of beetroot, and there's nothing stopping you from growing it yourself.

Nothing apart from getting your hands on the seed, that is. In the UK, it's only sold by a handful of specialist agricultural seed breeders and merchants, who don't bag it up in quantities small enough to suit most gardeners. Also, most of them are in East Anglia, which could make for a long looting run. Still, the sandy loam soil round there is perfect for beet-growing.

The industrial method of refining sugar beet – which uses carbon dioxide gas, soda ash, calcium hydroxide solution and a whole load of boiling and centrifuging – is hard to replicate in an end-of-society situation. But seeing as early nineteenth-century American farmers were quite capable of home-extracting sugar from the beets they grew using just heat, shallow drying pans and a screw press,[86] there's no reason you shouldn't do something similar. Like this:

- Wash the roots to remove all the muck, but don't peel them.
- Slice – or better, grate – the roots and put into a deep pot, with just enough water to cover them.
- Bring to a boil, then reduce the heat and simmer for at least an hour, or until the beets have completely softened.
- Remove the pot from the heat and allow to cool a little.
- Now you need to separate the liquid from the beets. You could try this by straining and squeezing through a muslin cloth. But if you have one, squishing the beets in an old-fashioned wooden apple press, the

HOW TO GROW SUGAR BEET

How many?	Four sugar beet plants will provide roots to make 1 kg of sugar.[85]
Rotation group	Neutral – but as sugar beet is more prone to diseases than ordinary beetroot, don't grow it on the same patch of ground for five years.
Where to grow	
Plants per m²	Ten
Sowing	From the second week of March until mid-April, sow seeds direct, 5 cm apart, into trenches of finely raked soil 2.5 cm deep and 40 cm apart. Draw the soil back over and keep moist until germination, then thin out gradually to 20 cm apart. Keep well weeded.
Feeding/ Watering	Add a high-P fertilizer to the site a couple of weeks before sowing. Use a high-N fertilizer immediately after sowing.
	Keep moist, not wet, until September.
Harvesting	The September after sowing, cut off and chuck the leafy tops. Dig up roots before the frosts begin. For maximum sugar yield, process ASAP.

kind with a screw-down lid, will give you more juice, faster.

- Next, get rid of the excess water. If you're in a hurry, reduce the juice over heat – carefully, it mustn't burn – in a saucepan until it's thick, dark and syrupy. Slower, but closer to how those beet farmers used to do it, is to pour the juice into wide, shallow pans, then leave it somewhere hot to evaporate, stirring regularly.

- Now you want to extract as much molasses – a blackish, sweetish but earthy-tasting goo – as possible. American farmers would squeeze the evaporated juices in a press, saving the molasses to cook with. In the twenty-first century, it'd be simpler to centrifuge the crystals out of the cooled liquid by running it through an electric juicer lined with muslin. But without either electricity or an apple press, use a salad spinner, also lined with muslin. Bash the plunger often enough and you can spin out a fair bit of liquid molasses.

- The muslin will now be lined with dark sugar solids. Lay this out to dry, then shake off and grind to powder with a rolling pin, or in a pestle and mortar.

And now – go make some jam.

Apple store

You'll remember that for safety reasons you have to save your looted 5 per cent acetic-acid vinegar for pickling vegetables. So what the heck will you sprinkle on your chips?

Thankfully, making vinegar is simple. Pretty much any weak, preservative-free solution of alcohol left in a warm place with access to oxygen will eventually, thanks to the action of Acetobacter bacteria, turn vinegary. But where, in an apocalypse, are you going to get all this alcohol from? Apples. Apples make cider, which makes apple cider vinegar. And in the British climate, apples are really easy to grow. Take a look at the instructions on the next page, and get planting.

Cider issue

Once you've harvested some apples, you can begin the fermenting process. Like this:

- Start by making a basic cider. Find a large glass container – nothing metal or plastic – and then fill it roughly halfway with apples cut into chunks. Don't peel them, though, as the skins are home to wild yeasts that will ferment the apples and produce alcohol.
- Put the chunks in the container,

and use a measuring jug to pour in enough cold water to fill the container to 5–10 cm from the brim. Keep track of how many litres you use.

- For every litre of water, add up to 50 g sugar, honey or molasses. This gives the yeasts a bit more than just the fruit sugars to get working on.
- Fermentation produces carbon dioxide gas, so cover the container loosely with a muslin cloth or a tea towel to let it escape. Put the container in a warmish place – ordinary room temperature is fine – and after a few days, you'll see bubbles beginning to rise and foam forming on the top. As you're not making proper get-pissed-at-the-bus-shelter cider, don't worry about skimming the foam off; just stir it back in.
- After seven to fourteen days, everything should smell alcoholic and cidery. Once it does, pour the liquid off into a second non-reactive container – that means glass or crockery.
- Now the yeasts have done their stuff, you want to encourage bacteria to turn the alcohol into acetic acid. The kind we have in mind need oxygen, warmth and darkness, so cover the container with your cloth again and store somewhere away from UV light at a temperature of 15–29° C.

HOW TO GROW APPLES

How many? One bush cider-apple tree on semi-vigorous (MM106) rootstock will provide enough apples to make eighteen litres of vinegar.[87]

Where to grow

Sowing To get crops quickly, choose a three-year-old, feathered maiden tree, either bare-root or in a pot. In the dormant season (November to March), dig a square hole that's as deep as the root ball and twice as wide, putting the soil you dig out to one side. Stand the tree in the hole so that the top of the root ball is level with the surrounding soil, and carefully shovel the set-aside soil back in, firming it gently around the roots as you go. Bang a strong wooden stake into the ground at a forty-five-degree angle – set it close to the trunk, but away from the root ball – and tie the trunk to it with something soft to stop the tree rocking in high winds. Water in with at least two cans of water.

Feeding Use a high-K fertilizer every January or February, spreading it from the trunk to the edge of the canopy. Follow with a high-N fertilizer every April. And keep an area of at least one square metre around the trunk weed-free, preferably by mulching with a thick layer of OM.

Watering For the first two summers, water weekly (one to two cans) in dry spells. After that, only water if drought threatens in midsummer.

Harvesting Depending on the variety you've planted, apples will be ready to pick from late summer on. Test by cupping a fruit in the palm of your hand and lifting it slightly upwards; if the stem separates easily from the tree, it's ready. The winter after harvesting, you'll need to prune. Which means going away and reading a book about fruit-tree pruning. Sorry.

▨ After four weeks, take a sniff. If the liquid doesn't smell strongly vinegary, put it back in the dark.

▨ Taste and/or smell every week. If at any point you see a cloudy disc forming on the surface of the liquid, celebrate: this is the vinegar mother, a floating slick of up to twenty different kinds of bacteria that work together to make acetic acid.

▨ As soon as any trace of alcohol taste and/or nail-polish smell is gone, scoop

Fruit from cider-apple trees will make the most drinkable cider, but as your aim is to make cider vinegar, a dessert-apple variety will still do the trick.

SURVIVAL PLAN

After all this, it may have occurred to you that preserving food demands a lot of time and resources you might not have. There is an alternative: good planning.

Every winter, draw a plan of your site, divide it into rotation groups and decide which crop you want to grow where. Then allot a higher proportion of space to crops that last for several months and don't need refrigeration to store safely: dried beans, for example, or root veg.

Next turn back to pages 180–3 and our rather wonderful Zombie Garden Calendar. Use the information there to create a sowing timetable which will allow for you to have some fresh veg that's harvestable year round. Sown and planted out at the right time, green leafy veg like kale and cabbage will keep the vitamins and fibre coming through the winter – without you needing to go anywhere near that lethal pickle jar. ✳

out the mother and put her into an airtight jar or bottle with just enough vinegar to cover her. Kept above 0° C, you can use her any time to kickstart your next batch of vinegar.

▪ Strain the remaining liquid several times through yet another clean muslin cloth. Pasteurize the vinegar in a stainless-steel or enamel pan by heating to 60° C for at least ten minutes, then pour into airtight, sterilized glass or crockery containers before storing.

FENCE JAM

You now know how preserving gluts of zombie-garden fruit and vegetables will be a lifesaver once the biters bite. There's also another option: using wild fruit, the kind you can forage for while waiting for your garden stocks to establish.

That word 'foraging', though. It so sounds like a long walk in damp woods with a woman called Leaf who believes in biodynamics. Luckily, there's plenty of food you can forage well away from the woods and from Leaf, and instead track down much nearer to the average urban home.

Blackberries are a pretty obvious place to start. But they are only around for a month in late summer, so we'd suggest widening the net and raiding office-block hedges, roundabout shrubs and carpark bushes for free jam- and jelly-friendly fruit.

Here's how.

1 FIND YOUR FRUIT

The kinds of fruit you'll be using all grow on so-called amenity plants: ultra-tough, cheap, no-bother shrubs and trees that councils and developers love to use to green-up drab outdoor spaces. **Crab apples** grow on the popular small street tree with the same name, planted for its masses of spring blossom. You'll find **silverberries** and **autumn olives** on evergreen elaeagnus, bushes that turn up a lot in suburban gardens. **Rosehips** are easy to find on apple rose, often used as a low hedging plant between bays in outdoor carparks. And **hawthorn berries or 'haws'** – well, everyone's seen a hawthorn hedge.

You'll need to pick roughly equal quantities of crab apples – these will provide the pectin that makes jams and jellies set solid – and at least one other fence fruit. As the apocalypse hasn't begun yet, check with any owners before you start to pick and, if you're not sure how to identify the right plants, use the handy table on page 207.

2 SIMMER TO A PULP

Once you've gathered your fruit, weigh the crab apples, then weigh out an equal amount of rosehips, hawthorn haws, silverberries or autumn olive. Wash, then cut off any stalks or brown bits of petal and slice in half. (Go carefully with rosehips: the insides are stuffed with fine hairs that can irritate your skin.)

Setting the crab apples aside, put the rest of the fruit in an enamel or stainless-steel pan (aluminium pans muck up the vitamin C) with enough water to cover them by a centimetre or so. Bring to a boil, then lower the heat and simmer until soft and pulpy. This might take up to two hours for rosehips, but other fruits will be ready much sooner. Then pulp the crab apples in the same way. This will take about fifteen minutes.

3 STRAIN OUT THE SEEDS

Now's the moment to decide whether you want to end up with a jam (cloudy, with bits) or a jelly (clear, no bits). Both taste the same, but you remove the inedible seeds from the fruit pulp in slightly different ways. For a clear jelly, mix the pulp of both fruits and use them to fill a jelly bag or a sieve lined with a muslin cloth. Leave above a bowl overnight to strain. For jam, either pass the mixed pulps in batches through a fine-holed food mill, or line a sieve with a muslin cloth and mash the pulp through with the back of a wooden spoon.

4 START THE JAM

Put a saucer in the fridge. (Trust us, this is relevant.) Then measure your strained juice or pulp. If you're making jelly, each litre of juice needs 700–800 g granulated sugar. For jam, every kilogram of pulp needs a kilogram of sugar – or maybe a little less, if you prefer your fruit flavours stronger. Either way, put your juice/pulp/sugar in a deep saucepan and stir over a low heat until the sugar has dissolved. Then turn up the heat and bring to a boil until your mix reaches 104° C. This is known as setting point: when sugar combines with pectin to make your jam/jelly firm and not a runny mess.

5 TEST THE SET

As you are not eighty years old and thus don't own a jam thermometer, after ten minutes check whether you've reached setting point by dropping a teaspoon of boiling mixture onto that cold saucer. (See?) Wait a minute, then push the dollop gently with your finger. If the surface stays smooth, let the jam/jelly boil a little longer, giving it a stir every now and again to make sure it doesn't burn. Do another dollop test: if the surface wrinkles, the jam/jelly is ready – turn off the heat and pour it straight into the jars. Close the lids tight, label the jars and eat the contents within a year.

6 PUSH THE BOUNDARIES

If you enjoyed doing this, expand your repertoire. Learn what a rowan tree (*Sorbus acuparia*) looks like, and turn its berries into rowan jelly to go with autumn roasts. Identify barberries (*Berberis vulgaris*) and use them to make zereshk, a key ingredient in Persian cuisine. Pick berries from the inevitable in-the-park elder bush (*Sambucus nigra*) and mix it with rosehips to make an immune-boosting syrup. And do all of this, but please – don't change your name to Leaf. ✳

HANDY TABLE NO. 15

PICK 'N' MIX

	IS IT A TREE OR A BUSH?	WHAT DO THE LEAVES LOOK LIKE?	WHAT DO THE FLOWERS LOOK LIKE?	WHAT DOES THE FRUIT LOOK LIKE?
CRAB APPLE *Malus sylvestris*	Small tree	Green, oval, usually pointed at the ends, with finely toothed edges	Pink, white or red blossoms that appear in mid-spring	Red, yellow or green, hanging on long stalks; about the size of cherries, but with little brown poky-out bits at the ends; cores are star-shaped, like apples'
APPLE ROSE *Rosa rugosa*	Small, very prickly bush	Matt green, small, oval, finely toothed and deeply ridged	Dark pink or white, look like flat, papery roses. Flowers appear in early summer	Oval, deep red and shiny, stuck on the ends of twigs
SILVERBERRY *Elaeagnus x ebbingei*	Large evergreen bush	Oval, slightly crinkly edged, very dark green or green and bright yellow; undersides are silvery	Small, creamy, scented, bell-shaped flowers, which appear in autumn	Bunches of what look like small olives along the lengths of branches; start off green and silvery, turn brownish red and speckled when ripe, usually around February
AUTUMN OLIVE *Elaeagnus umbellata*	Large evergreen bush/ small tree	Similar to silverberry, but longer, slimmer and more silvered	Like silverberry, but flowers in May	Round, bright red, speckled and currant-sized, ripens in autumn
HAWTHORN *Crataegus monogyna*	Bush/ small tree	Mid-green, look like miniature versions of oak leaves	Masses of white five-petalled flowers in May	Round, dark crimson and pea-sized, in clusters on ends of twigs

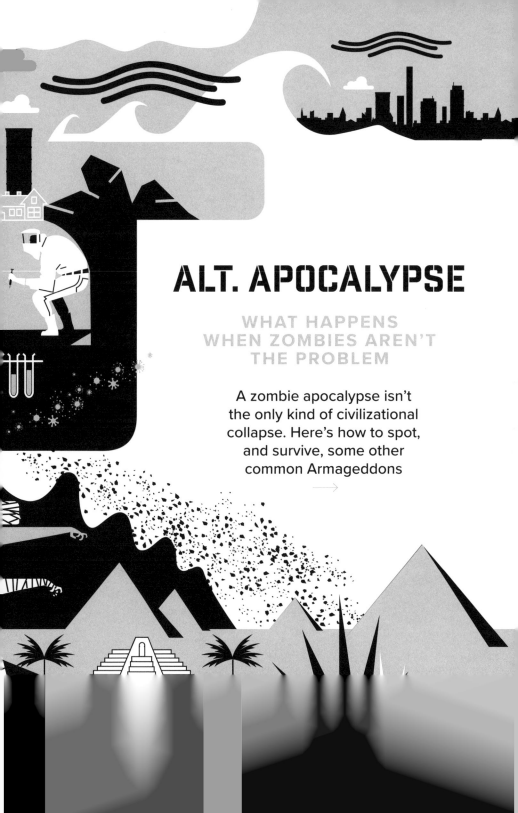

ALT. APOCALYPSE

WHAT HAPPENS WHEN ZOMBIES AREN'T THE PROBLEM

A zombie apocalypse isn't the only kind of civilizational collapse. Here's how to spot, and survive, some other common Armageddons

→

Uncontrolled escape of a man-made virus

- Starts in a secret animal laboratory staffed by well-meaning liberal and/or arrogant scientists
- It's very catching
- Can be survived if one of the scientists finds and is forced to look after a special child who has the antibodies
- Defeating the man-made virus, and adopting the special child, will sort out the scientist's marriage problems

Alien invasion

- Starts as a result of radio transmissions beamed into space by well-meaning liberal and/or arrogant scientists
- The alien invaders blow up a series of iconic buildings with a giant laser beam fired from their giant spacecraft
- They can be defeated with the help of a single wise-cracking maverick scientist
- Defeating the alien invasion will sort out the maverick scientist's marriage problems

Rebirth of ancient and malevolent god

- Starts when his/her tomb has been disturbed, after millennia, by a maverick archaeologist
- This kind of apocalypse only kills Nazi soldiers and/or cowardly local guides
- Can be survived by closing the portal to another dimension before something unspeakable bursts out
- Or by opening the portal to another dimension so that something unspeakable gets sucked in
- Defeating the ancient and malevolent god sorts out everyone's marriage problems

Climate change such that the earth's atmosphere warms by greater than 2°C

- Starts soon after the Industrial Revolution
- Accelerates after an ancient and malevolent president is voted into office
- Will be hard to survive, though zombie gardening will help
- Has no positive impact on divorce rates

EPILOGUE:
THE BEGINNING

There aren't many good things to be said for a zombie apocalypse, but here's one: they don't last for ever.

Zombies are made of flesh and bone, and that means they rot. Give it five years or so, and the combined efforts of bacteria, fungi and flesh-eating maggots will have reduced the number of still-walking walking dead to practically zero.

Now what? You, of course, will not only still be alive but, after five years of healthy eating, positively kicking. Your zombie garden will be well established, protected from pests and with a rich soil full of microorganisms, worms and organic matter. Five years of sowing and planting will have given you a good understanding of how to get the best out of your key veg-garden crops. By now you'll be getting some decent harvests from any fruit bushes or trees you planted. And you'll have a good idea of how to grow and store food without relying too much on fossil fuels, either for preserving or for fertilization.

Clearly it's time for you to get out there and help rebuild society – not least because the economics of growing food without machinery means larger groups will have more to eat. It may or may not take a village to raise a child, but it definitely takes a hamlet to hand-reap, thresh and winnow five acres of wheat. So now is the moment to make peace with that rival settlement. Then draw up a work rota.

But also, we'd argue, it's time to do more gardening. Now that you don't have to concentrate on basic nutrition, there's a whole world of other crops out there that you can experiment with.

How about growing your own booze, for instance? The end of the world is a fabulous excuse for a party. That would mean planting hops, grape vines, juniper and all kinds of herbs for flavouring gin. And if you're already growing wheat, you've got the makings of a *weissbier* right there.

Or you could add some gourmet crops to your garden layout. Asparagus is one of the loveliest things to eat cut fresh from the ground, the fruit of a mulberry one of the loveliest to eat fresh from the tree.

To keep things sustainable into the post-zombie future, you could expand your permanent plantings, mixing in forest-garden plants such as bamboo for shoots, lime trees for salad leaves, stone pine for pine nuts or white currants for, er, white currants.

Or you could hark back to those merry hipster days before the biters bit and grow micro-herbs, oriental leaves and, if you've got a nice warm spot, some soya beans with which to make a nostalgic soy-milk latte, two shots, to go. Though admittedly you'd have to do without the two shots. Even the most skilled zombie gardener can't grow coffee plants in this country.

The exciting thing is this: there are so many plants out there, each of them different, each of them in its own way fascinating and challenging, that it is a life's work to learn to grow them all. More than a life's work, in fact.

> There's a world of other crops out there to experiment with

So don't hang about. Now the zombies are gone, get out there and track down other zombie gardeners. Ask if they'll let you visit their gardens – you'll see something new in every plot. Swap seeds with them, swap plants with them and above all swap stories with them. Gardening books are all very well but – and forgive us for waiting until the end of our book to say this – the best way to learn about gardening is to listen to other gardeners. Open your ears to what they have to tell you about their experiences, and share with them what you've discovered about how to sow, grow and stay alive. We can guarantee you'll have some fun.

What do you do when the zombies have staggered off over the horizon and into history? You grab a fork. And then you get gardening.

RESOURCES

Everwilde Farms
PO Box 40, Sand Creek, WI 54765 USA
(+1 888 848 3837); everwilde.com
Sells and ships packets of open-pollinated (OP) sugar beet seed to gardeners in the UK – though brace yourself for the import duties.

FELCO
Stockists via felco.com/uk_en/dealers/find
Not the cheapest secateurs and garden knives out there, but some of the best; plus the (Swiss) manufacturer sells spares for all its products, so you can replace bits when they fall off/break/get lost.

Franchi Seeds of Italy
Phoenix Business Centre, Unit D2, Rosslyn Crescent, Harrow, Middlesex HA1 2SP
(020 8427 5020); seedsofitaly.com
Online food/gardening catalogue that specializes in Italian fruit and veg seed, including packets of bread-making winter wheat seed – of an unnamed variety, but it grows well in British conditions.

Gardenfocused.co.uk
Warwickshire-based blogger who's created a free, simple but very clever tool that allows you to create a sowing and planting calendar with timings based on your local climate.

Garden Organic
Ryton Gardens, Wolston Lane, Coventry, Warwickshire CV8 3LG (024 7630 3517);
gardenorganic.org.uk
Long-standing organic gardening-research foundation and educational charity. Has a useful 'what to do this month' section on its website, and also offers members the chance to pick six free packets of seed annually from its Heritage Seed Library, including some fascinating landrace varieties suitable for unusual growing conditions.

The Garlic Farm
Mersley Farm, Mersley Lane, Newchurch, Isle of Wight, PO36 0NR (01983 865378);
thegarlicfarm.co.uk
Sells a mail-order range of seed garlic varieties (including elephant garlic), all of which are suitable for growing in the UK climate. The website also has some good variety-specific growing advice and explains how to plait garlic into ropes for storage. Not that plaiting garlic is something you ever thought you'd do.

Orange Pippin Trees
33 Algarth Rise, Pocklington, York YO42 2HX
(01759 392007); orangepippintrees.co.uk
Mail-order fruit-tree specialist which sells, among other things, cordon-trained trees for growing in containers. The website offers some helpful services, including a tree-finder questionnaire and a pollination-group checker.

The Real Seed Catalogue
PO Box 18, Newport near Fishguard, Pembrokeshire SA65 0AA (01239 821107);
realseeds.co.uk
Sells a large and interesting range of unusual OP veg seed; the website also carries some useful (and money-saving) veg-by-veg advice on collecting and storing your own seed.

Victoriana Nursery Gardens
Challock, Ashford, Kent TN25 4DG (01233 740529);
victoriananursery.co.uk
Offers an unusual range of tomato seed, including lots of OP varieties that are suitable for outdoor growing.

Vital Seeds
Westford Farm, Drewsteignton, Exeter, EX6 6RD
(01647 281 288); vitalseeds.co.uk
A new but useful organic OP seed specialist, with a smaller range than the Real Seed Catalogue but of (mostly) better-known, more widely used varieties. Tags relevant stock as 'suitable for containers', which is helpful.

Owen Bush
Bushfire Forge, East Wickham Farm, Wickham St, Welling, Kent DA16 3DA
07973 798690; owenbush.co.uk
One of a handful of highly skilled British artist-blacksmiths who specialize in swords, Bush makes hand-forged Japanese katana-style blades that are perfect for keeping zombies off your broccoli – and also very, very beautiful.

Leszek Sikon
Kingdom Forge, Manor Barns, The Street, Brundish, Woodbridge, Suffolk IP13 8BL; lsikonblacksmith.com
If you'd rather concentrate more on growing and less on zombie killing, the blade- and blacksmith Leszek Sikon forges superb, made-to-order farming implements out of ex-World War Two ammunition. Which, in an apocalypse, feels just right.

FURTHER READING

Hen Keeping, *Mike Hatcher (New Holland Publishers, 2009)*
If you've paid attention to page 188 and now want to add hens to your zombie garden, who better than a man called Hatcher to guide you? Also, he really knows what he's talking about.

How to Grow Winter Vegetables, *Charles Dowding (Green Books, 2011)*
Charles Dowding is Britain's leading no-dig evangelist, as well as being a fabulous gardener who will definitely survive the apocalypse. And of all the veg-growing guides in our collection, his is the stone-cold best (see what we did?) on getting through the hungry gap. Actually – just make that the best, full stop.

The Market Gardener: A Successful Grower's Handbook for Small-Scale Organic Farming, *J.M. Fortier (New Society Publishers, 2014)*
While we're on the subject of gardeners clever enough to make it through Armageddon, do read this book. The skill-level is quite advanced – and Fortier recommends using more machinery than you might have to hand – but his mastery of maximizing yields from small spaces is worth paying attention to.

Not on the Label: What Really Goes Into the Food on Your Plate, *Felicity Lawrence (Penguin, 2004; revised 2013)*
If you found our few factettes about food security and the potential precariousness of the supply chain in the intro interesting, this is where to go for a much fuller story – plus an update on the horror show of the horsemeat scandal.

Seed to Seed: Seed Saving and Growing Techniques for Vegetable Gardeners, *Suzanne Ashworth (Seed Savers Exchange, 2002)*
A detailed, highly knowledgeable guide to saving and storing seed of 160 common vegetable plants. Written for an American audience – but listen, they need books too.

Small-Scale Grain Raising, *Gene Logsdon (Chelsea Green, 1977; second edition 2009)*
Just a lovely read, even if you never plan to grow sorghum and corn on an acre in Ohio. Logsdon chats away like you're his favourite neighbour, and he teaches you loads while he's at it.

RHS Pruning and Training, *Christopher Brickell and David Joyce (Dorling Kindersley, 1996)*
RHS Vegetable & Fruit Gardening, *ed. Michael Pollock (Dorling Kindersley, 2002; revised 2012)*
Every year the Royal Horticultural Society fills shelves with new gardening books, lots of them jolly and bright. But our favourites are both deeply boring – because they're extremely detailed, and therefore actually useful. *Pruning and Training* will show you how to get proper crops out of fruit bushes and trees, and *V&F Gardening* has the most comprehensive chapter we've come across on garden pests and diseases.

Vinegar: The User-Friendly Standard Text Reference and Guide to Appreciating, Making, and Enjoying Vinegar, *Lawrence J. Diggs (Authors Choice Press, 2000)*
There won't be much to do in the apocalypse except make vinegar, so we'd suggest you give this a thorough read.

The Walking Dead, Volumes 1–31, *Robert Kirkman, Tony Moore & Charlie Adlard (Image Comics, 2003 to present)*
What, we need to say why?

REFERENCES

Introduction and Chapter 1: The End

1 Based on content of 100 g of raw fruit or vegetable and an average GDR for men and women aged nineteen to sixty-four

2 Unless otherwise stated, figures given are the average of those in *RHS Vegetable & Fruit Gardening*, ed. Michael Pollock (Dorling Kindersley, revised edition 2012) and *The RHS Allotment Handbook* (Mitchell Beazley, 2010), plus (when relevant) 80 per cent of average of yields from 2013–17 as published by the Department for Environment, Food and Rural Affairs (DEFRA) in two of its annual publications: *Agriculture in the United Kingdom* 2017 (AUK17), September 2018, and 'Horticultural Statistics Dataset' (HSD), December 2018

3 *AUK17*

4 Based on ITC Trade Map/United Nations Comtrade Database figures for 2017

5 Based on figures from a) Agriculture and Horticulture Development Board (AHDB), Oct. 2017 – milk for direct human consumption only; b) British Egg Industry Council 2018, and assuming suppliers hold up to four weeks of stock; c) 'UK Horticultural Statistics'; d) Quadram Institute, 2017; e) British Tomato Growers' Association, 2017

6 There are approximately 14,155 supermarket outlets in the UK, serving a population of approximately 60 million

7 Based on Tesco PLC figures for 2017 and the average disposable plastic shopping bag holding 5 kg of groceries

8 As given in the UK Government's *Digest of UK Energy Statistics (DUKES) 2017*

Chapter 2: The Plot Thickens

9 *Hansard*, HC Deb, 19 April 1917, vol. 92, c1878W

10 Excerpted from *Allotments for All: The Story of a Great Movement*, by Gerald W. Butcher, National Union of Allotment Holders (George Allen & Unwin, 2017)

11 *Housing Space Standards*, Greater London Authority, 2006; london.gov.uk

12 Based on average yield of 3.2 kg fruit per plant, three plants per 100 x 40 cm growbag, and 2 kg of fruit making 500 ml passata

13 Horticultural Trade Association 'Market Update 2015'/Ipsos MORI survey of GB adults (conducted 2014)

14 Based on 80 per cent of average yields 2013–2017, *AUK17*; and bread loaves requiring 500 g wholemeal flour

15 Housing SpaceStandards

16 Data from landis.org.uk/soilscapes/

17 Met Office annual average for Shanklin climate station, 1981–2010

18 Michigan State University Extension, 'Growing Blueberries in the Home Garden'

Chapter 3: Gardening is War

19 Based on USDA Food Composition Databases and a) RHS 'Trials Report, Maincrop Potato', 1993 or b) average of 80 per cent yields per acre, 'HSD', and average of yields and plants per square metre, *RHS Allotment Handbook* and *RHS Vegetable & Fruit Gardening* or c) average of RHS figures

20 Based on 66 per cent of fresh yield

21 Based on 66 per cent of podded yield; drying information supplied by Hodmedod's British Pulses and Grains, hodmedods.co.uk

22 Based on podded yield of 1.5 kg beans per plant from fifteen plants in a square metre, Mitchell Beazley, *RHS Allotment Handbook*

23 Based on 11 per cent of average fresh yield

24 Average of yields for spring, summer, autumn and winter cabbage

25 Based on average nutrients for 100 g raw cabbage and 100 g raw red cabbage, USDA Food Composition Databases

26 Based on average yields per plant/per square metre, Heather Bryant, 'Winter Squash Trial', University of New Hampshire, 2011

27 Assuming a single plant yields twenty leaves weighing 14 g each, and using average of plants per square metre in Pollock, *RHS Vegetable & Fruit Gardening*, and B. Gélinas and P. Seguin, 'Development and Yield Potential of Grain Amaranth in Southwestern Québec', *Canadian Journal of Plant Science*, 2008, 88:133–6

28 Based on 33 per cent of leaf yield from perpetual spinach/leaf beet

29 Based on per plant yield of 9 g (authors' measurements) and average sixty plants per square metre, Pollock, *RHS Vegetable & Fruit Gardening*, and Mitchell Beazley, *RHS Allotment Handbook*

30 R. Harmer, N. Straw and D. Williams, 'Boar, Bluebells and Beetles', *Quarterly Journal of Forestry*, 2011, 105:195–202; 'Wild Boar and Deer in the Forest of Dean', *Forest Research*, Agency of the Forestry Commission, 2014

31 D. M. Glen, C. W. Wiltshire, D. A. Bohan, 'The Abundance and Population Size Structure of *Deroceras reticulatum* and Other Pest Slug Species in Arable Fields', *Integrated Slug Control in Arable Crops Project Report*, Home Grown Cereals Authority for DEFRA, 2006, 74–91

32 Rapeseed yields based on average 1,600 litres per hectare, 'Pure Plant Oil Facts', ETP BioEnergy, www.etpbioenergy.eu, and Union for the Promotion of Oil and Protein Plants, www.ufop.de

33 'Pure Plant Oil Facts'

34 *United Kingdom Housing Energy Fact File*, Department of Energy and Climate Change, 2013

35 *Energy Conservation in the Mechanical Forest Industries*, FAO, Forestry Paper 93, Rome, 1990

36 'Yield Models for Energy Coppice of Poplar and Willow', Volume A, *Forest Research*, Department of Trade and Industry, 2005

37 S. J. Hodge, 'Forestry Commission Bulletin 99: Urban Trees, a Survey of Street Trees in England', Department of the Environment Arboriculture Contract, 1991

38 Based on 80 per cent of yields in *AUK17*

39 C. A. White, R. Sylvester-Bradley, P. M. Berry, 'Root-length Densities of UK Wheat and Oilseed Rape Crops with Implications for Water Capture and Yield', *Journal of Experimental Botany*, 2015, 66(8):2293–2303

40 Based on a recommended agricultural sowing rate of 325 seeds per square metre, 95 per cent germination rate and average seed weight of 50 g per 1,000 seeds. Rates and weights provided by Elsom Seeds Ltd, Lincolnshire, 01775 71500

41 I. Photiades, A. Hadjichristodoulou, 'Sowing Date, Sowing Depth, Seed Rate and Row Spacing of Wheat and Barley Under Dryland Conditions', *Field Crops Research* 9, 1984

42 *Winter Wheat Guide*, Irish Agriculture and Food Development Authority (TEAGASC), 2016

Chapter 4: Soldier Skills

43 R. Stobart, N. L. Morris, H. Hinton, H. Fielding, C. Stoate, 'Evaluation of Sustainable Soil Management and Cover Crop Practices', presented at the European Society of Agronomy (ESA) 14, Edinburgh, 2016

44 Based on an average half-life of thirty-one days for carbon mineralization of incorporated catch crops, S. Kuo, U. M. Sanju, E. J. Jellum, 'Winter Cover Crop Effects on Soil Organic Carbon and Carbohydrate in Soil', *Soil Science Society of America Journal*, 1997, 61:145–52

45 L. Köhl, F. Oehl, M. G. A. Van Der Heijde, 'Agricultural Practices Indirectly Influence Plant

Productivity and Ecosystem Services Through Effects on Soil Biota', *Ecological Applications*, 2014, 24(7):1842–53

46 Dr A. H. Free, H. M. Free, *Urinalysis in Clinical Laboratory Practice* (CRC Press, 1975)

47 T. S. Griffin, 'Using Wood Ash on Your Farm', University of Maine Extension Bulletin

48 *Winter Wheat Guide*, TEAGASC

49 J. P. Chastain, J. J. Camberato, P. Skewes, 'Poultry Manure Production and Content', *Clemson University Confined Animal Manure Managers (CAMM) Poultry Training Manual 2001.*

50 J. P. Chastain, K. Moore, 'Plant Nutrient and Carbon Content of Equine Manure as Influenced by Stall Management in South Carolina', Clemson University, 2014

51 'Nutrient Value of Compost', University of California, Davis, OSFM Symposium 2009

52 C. C. Delwiche, J. Wijler, 'Non-Symbiotic Nitrogen Fixation in Soil', *Plant and Soil*, 1956, 7(2):113–129

53 M. Silgram, R. Harrison, 'The Mineralisation of Nitrogen in Cover Crops: A Review', Annex 1 to *MAFF Final Report (NT 1508)*, Ministry of Agriculture, Food and Fisheries, 1998

54 B. Cupina et al., 'Winter Cover Crops as Green Manure in a Temperate Region: The Effect on Nitrogen Budget and Yield of Silage Maize', *Crop & Pasture Science*, 2017, 68:1060–9

55 R. Stobart et al., 'Evaluation of Sustainable Soil Management'; C. J. E. Fowler, L. M. Condron, R. D. Mclenaghen, 'Effects of Green Manures on Nitrogen Loss and Availability in an Organic Cropping System', *New Zealand Journal of Agricultural Research*, 2004, 47:95–100

56 Based on USDA analyses and information supplied by the Nutrient Company, www.thenutrientcompany.com

57 USDA Agricultural Research Service, 1992–2016; Dr. Duke's Phytochemical and Ethnobotanical Databases

58 B. Bareeba, W. O. Odwongo, J. S. Mugerwa, 'The Potential of Russian Comfrey as an Animal Feedstuff in Uganda', *Proceedings of the Joint Feed Resources Networks Workshop*, 1991

59 K. R. Sanderson, J. Sanderson, 'Potassium Management for Carrots in Prince Edward Island', *Canadian Journal of Plant Science*, 2006, 86:1405–7; 'Crop Guide: Strawberries', Haifa Group; 'Potassium Requirements of Crops', Proceedings of the 11th Congress International Potash Institute, 1978, 225–342

60 P. Schramel, G. Lill, S. Hasse, 'Mineral and Trace Elements in Human Urine', *Journal of Clinical Chemistry and Clinical Biochemistry*, 1985, 23:293–301

61 F. L. Walley, G. W. Clayton, P. R. Miller, P. M. Carr, G. P. Lafond, 'Nitrogen Economy of Pulse Production in the Northern Great Plains, *Agronomy Journal*, 2007, 99:1710–18

62 X. Jiang, J. Morgan, M. P. Doyle, 'Fate of Escherichia coli O157:H7 in Manure-Amended Soil', *Applied Environmental Microbiology*, 2002, 68:2605–9

Chapter 5: The Groundwork

63 RHS 'Trials Report, Maincrop Potato'

64 Based on dry yield as 66 per cent of average fresh yields

65 Based on double cropping, i.e. picking half beans fresh and leaving half to dry

66 R. Bressani, E. C. de Martell, C. M. de Godínez, 'Protein Quality Evaluation of Amaranth in Adult Humans', *Plant Foods for Human Nutrition*, 1993, 43(2):123–43

67 Based on seed yields of 25 g per plant (B. Gélinas, P. Seguin, 'Development and Yield Potential') and twenty leaves weighing 14 g each per plant

68 Based on dry yields as 11 per cent of average fresh yield

69 W. Song, C. M. Derito, M. Keshu Liu, X. He, M. Dong, R. H. Liu, 'Cellular Antioxidant Activity of Common Vegetables', *Journal of Agricultural and Food Chemistry*, 2010, 58(11):6621–9

70 Assuming double cropping, i.e. taking some leaves from plants, then harvesting roots; figures given are based on average yield of roots from beetroot varieties and 33 per cent of average yield of leaves from leaf-beet varieties

71 Based on average yields from Pollock, *RHS Vegetable & Fruit Gardening*, Beazley, *RHS Allotment Gardening*, and Heather Bryant, 'Winter Squash Trial'

72 S. Ferreira, R. Boley, 'Cucumber Mosaic Virus', University of Hawaii Entomology and Pest Management Extension

73 S. N. H. Gadel-Hak, Y. M. M. Moustafa, G. F. Abdel-Naem, I. Abdel-Wahab, 'Studying Different Quantitative and Qualitative Traits of Some White- and Colored-Bulb Garlic Genotypes Grown Under a Drip Irrigation System', *Australian Journal of Basic and Applied Sciences*, 2015, 5:1415–27

74 Ph. Vivekanandini Devi, Dr J. K. Brar, 'Comparison of Proximate Composition and Mineral Concentration of Allium ampeloprasum (elephant garlic) and Allium sativum (garlic)', India *Chemical Science Review and Letters*, 2018, 7(25):362–7

75 B. G. Hughes, L. D. Lawson, 'Antimicrobial Effects of *Allium sativum* L. (garlic), *Allium ampeloprasum* L. (elephant garlic), and *Allium cepa* L. (onion), Garlic Compounds and Commercial Garlic Supplement Products' *Phytotherapy Research*, 1991, 5(4):154–8; V. Lanzotti, F. Scala, G. Bonanomi, 'Compounds from Allium Species with Cytotoxic and Antimicrobial Activity', *Phytochemistry Reviews*, 2014, 13:769–91

76 Md. H. Rahman, M. S. Haque, M. Ahmed, 'Pre-planting Temperature Treatments for Breaking Dormancy of Garlic Cloves', *Asian Journal of Plant Sciences*, 2003, 2:123–6; M. D. Dufoo-Hurtado, J. Á. Huerta-Ocampo, A. Barrera-Pacheco, A. P. Barba de la Rosa, E. M. Mercado-Silva, 'Low Temperature Conditioning of Garlic (*Allium sativum L.*) "Seed" Cloves Induces Alterations in Sprouts Proteome', *Frontiers in Plant Science*, 2016, 201(6):332

77 Based on average of early and maincrop yields

78 Average of nutrients in 100 g raw cabbage and 100 g raw red cabbage, both USDA Food Databases

79 Based on a medium pasture-stocking rate of 1.5 livestock units (LU) per hectare, LU per animal as given in J. Nix, *Farm Management Pocketbook* 34th Edition (Imperial College Press, 2004), for one male and one female animal, except a) one hen per square metre and b) one animal, plus 100 m^2 of land to grow cereal crops on

80 Based on stocking rates as above and c) five-year average yield 7,652 litres per cow per annum, Agriculture and Horticulture Development Board, 2018; d) daily output of 1.4 litres per ewe, G. Geenty, 'Dairy and Suckled Milk Production of Dorset Ewes', *New Zealand Journal of Experimental Agriculture*, 1980, 8:3–4, 191–7; e) 800 litres per goat per annum, Irish Agriculture and Food Development Authority, 'Dairy Goats Fact Sheet', May 2006; f) per hen, based on 260 eggs per hen per annum, 'The Life of Laying Hens', Compassion in World Farming; g) 80 per cent average winter wheat yield, AUK17

81 Based on stocking rates as above, and NPK g per kg solid-matter manure per animal per year, J. C. Barker, S. C. Hodges, F. R. Walls, 'Livestock Manure Production Rates and Nutrient Content', *North Carolina Agrichemicals Manual,* North Carolina Department of Agriculture & Consumer Services, 2002

82 G. E. Welbaum, 'Annual Culture of Globe Artichoke from Seed in Virginia', *Horticultural Technology*, April–June 1994, 4(2):147–9

Chapter 6: Self-preservation

83 J. McLauchlin, K. A. Grant, C. L. Little, 'Food-borne Botulism in the United Kingdom', *Journal of Public Health*, 2006, 28(4):337–42

84 P. Baker (PRB Associates Limited) and A. Morgan (Global 78 Limited), 'Final Annex Report 9: UK Sugar Imports', *Resilience of the Food Supply to Port Disruption* (DEFRA, 2012)

85 Based on recommended agricultural drill rate of 100,000 plants per hectare, 80 per cent average yields, AUK17, and sugar yields per hectare, C. M. Hoffmann and C. Kenter, 'Yield Potential of Sugar Beet – Have We Hit the Ceiling?', *Frontiers in Plant Science*, 2018, 9:289

86 J. Nicholson, *The Farmer's Assistant, Being a Digest of All That Relates to Agriculture, and the Conducting of Rural Affairs; Alphabetically Arranged, and Adapted for the United States* (B. Warner, 1820)

87 Based on average 27 kg yields for semi-vigorous bush apple varieties requiring 9 m^2 space, Pollock, *RHS Vegetable & Fruit Gardening*, and Chris Bowers' apple-planting guide; plus 15 kg of apples producing ten litres cider

INDEX

ACKNOWLEDGEMENTS

 First, we'd like to thank Martin Toseland, Ellen Parnavelas and Diana Beaumont, all of whom understood that the apocalypse could happen and that vegetables will help. This book wouldn't exist without them.

Our gratitude too to the team at Head of Zeus: Stephanie Mitchell for keeping things accurate; Heather Ryerson and Jessie Price for making it all look exciting, even the boring bits; and Christian Wood, for his witty and deeply enjoyable illustrations. When the apocalypse comes, let's hope it looks like this.

We're also grateful to everyone who generously answered silly questions such as 'Could a zombie shut down a nuclear power station?' These include but aren't restricted to: the Agriculture & Horticulture Development Board; the British Geological Survey; the British Growers Association; Claire Hargreaves at British Sugar; the British Tomato Growers' Association; Paolo Salcedo at DEFRA; Elsoms Seeds Ltd; the Food & Drink Federation; Josiah Meldrum at Hodmedod's British Pulses & Grains; Greencell; Sarah Revell at National Grid; NFB Import; the Quadram Institute; the Real Seed Catalogue; Guy Barter at the Royal Horticultural Society; Sophie Morgan at the Soil Association; and Mark Culloden at Strube UK.

Over the years we've learnt from many food growers wiser and more skilled than us, who've helped with advice and only the occasional sad shake of the head. Our particular thanks to Catherine Birkett, Simon Kunath, and of course Nigel Scott-Harden and Alain Miaule, who planted the seed.

Thank you too to Katharine Lloyd, Hazel, Jack and Tom Clarke for the love and support; to Tyber Thomas for the heavy lifting; to Simon Walker for putting us in the picture; to Sharn Matharu at Various Artists Ltd for keeping the bigger game going; and to Mirren Gidda for the first read, plus not telling us it was actual rubbish.

Finally, thank you to Robert Kirkman and the late George A. Romero. You can bet they never expected this.

THE END*

* of the book. But not of the world